THE LIFE AND WORK

OF WILHELM REICH

THE LIFE AND WORK

Translated from the French by
GHISLAINE BOULANGER

OF WILHELM REICH

MICHEL CATTIER

HORIZON PRESS   NEW YORK

To Denise Schwarb

This work was first published in the French language in 1969 under the title *La Vie et l'Oeuvre du Docteur Wilhelm Reich* by Editions L'Age d'Homme S.A. Lausanne.

Library of Congress Catalog Card No. 76-171016
ISBN 0-8180-0220-4
Manufactured in the United States of America

Contents

Chapter I

The Meeting with Freud

Wilhelm Reich was born on March 24, 1897, in Galicia, a region situated in the eastern confines of the Austro-Hungarian Empire[1] and inhabited by a mixture of Germans, Poles, Jews and Ukrainians. (Today it is divided between Poland and the Soviet Union.) Reich's family were well-to-do German-speaking farmers. Between the ages of six and ten, he was taught by a tutor hired by his father; he then went to the German *Gymnasium,* where he obtained his first natural-science diploma in 1915.

Reich's interest in the natural sciences was aroused early: at the age of eight, he started collecting plants and insects in order to observe their modes of reproduction; he also did his share of work in the fields each summer. In 1914, when his father died, Reich took over the farm management for a year, while he continued his studies. In 1915 he entered the Austrian Army, and at the war's end he was a lieutenant. Having lost all his possessions in the defeat, he enrolled in 1918 in the Faculty of Medi-

---

[1]He kept his Austrian nationality until 1938.

cine at the University of Vienna, and paid his way by giving private lessons, leading an austere existence, "neither frequenting the local cafés nor attending social gatherings . . ."

In the first pages of his book *The Function of the Orgasm,* Reich tells how he began devouring books on general biology, sexology and philosophy after he had been demobilized. The arguments (which no longer concern us today) between those who embraced a mechanist view of life on the one hand and those with a mystical viewpoint on the other, fascinated Reich. The mechanists held that living organisms are ruled entirely by the laws of physical chemistry, or by extrapolations of these laws. The mystics believed in a mysterious life force that fundamentally differentiated living beings from machines. Reich maintains that he sympathized with both theories, but believed that they both left something to be desired. He felt that living beings were not machines; at the same time the explanation offered by the mystics seemed wordy and idealistic to him. Twenty years later he was certain he had overcome this contradiction through his discovery of the "orgone."

In January 1919, Reich attended a sexological seminar which led him to study numerous works on sexuality; and, during the summer, he wrote a paper on the concept of the libido from Forel to Jung.

On March 1 of the same year, he had noted in his journal:

Perhaps my own morality objects to it. However, from my own experience, and from observation of myself and others, I have become convinced that sexuality is the center around

which revolves the whole of social life as well
as the inner life of the individual.[2]

The discovery of Freud's work and the distinction Freud made between sexuality and procreation
aroused Reich's interest and determined his choice
of a profession. Hitherto sexuality had been looked
upon as the propagation instinct; but Freud showed
that sexual instincts are present in infants, that they
pass through several phases as they advance to-
toward the genital stage, and that perversions such
as fetishism or sadism have sexual overtones. In dis-
associating sexuality from the function of reproduction, Freud was flying in the face of traditional
bourgeois concepts which held that sexuality awoke
with puberty at the time when the individual became capable of breeding offspring. In anatomy and
physiology, the sexual organs were described as apparatus whose sole function was reproduction.

Permeated as it was with finalism and strict
morality, sexology rested on such ambiguous notions
as the reproduction instinct or the maternal instinct.

At the end of 1919, Reich was elected leader of
the sexological seminar, where sexual sociology, en-
docrinology, the physiology and anatomy of the genital organs and especially psychoanalysis were studied. At this juncture in his career, he paid his first
visit to Freud which he describes in *The Function
of the Orgasm:*

> Freud spoke to me like an ordinary human be-
> ing. He had piercingly intelligent eyes; they did
> not try to penetrate the listener's eyes in a
> visionary pose; they simply looked into the

[2]*The Function of the Orgasm* (New York: Farrar,
Straus & Cudahy, 1961), p. 4.

world, straight and honest. He asked about our work in the seminar and thought it was very sensible. We were right, he said, and it was a pity that there was no interest in the subject of sexuality, or, if there was any, only a false one. He would be glad to help us out with literature. He knelt in front of his bookshelves and got out some books and pamphlets . . . His manner of speaking was quick, to the point, and lively. The movements of his hands were natural. Everything he did and said was shot through with tints of irony. I had come there in a state of trepidation and left with a feeling of pleasure and friendliness. That was the starting point of fourteen years of intensive work in and for psychoanalysis.[3]

In October 1920, Reich, still a medical student, became a member of the Vienna Psychoanalytic Society. His first published work appeared that year in *Zeitschrift für Sexualwissenschaft* (*The Journal of Sexology*).

It was also at this time that Reich began treating patients, applying Freud's directives to the letter. The patient, lying on a couch with the analyst behind him, was obliged to say everything that was going through his mind. He recounted his dreams that then had to be broken down into sequences to which he was asked to furnish associations. All the material was interpreted as it was presented. Reich immediately ran into technical difficulties. He had the impression that his patients never let themselves go entirely, or that they conformed too willingly to his demands, which was an even more subtle way of evading him. He occasionally came across patients

---

[3]*Ibid.*, p. 17.

who were so inhibited that they remained silent for hours. Theoretically it was known that the patients were defending themselves against unconscious elements and that these resistances must be broken down. Reich turned to his more experienced colleagues for advice but they told him to be patient and to continue to analyze in the face of all difficulties.

The resistances that his patients raised put serious obstacles in the way of a cure. For years resistances had been recognized as a sign of repression; but no systematic technique existed to overcome them, unless it was to remind the patient to stick to the fundamental rule (to express all ideas that came into his head without censoring them or holding any back). Reich was also confused by an apparent contradiction in the therapeutic outcome: when a neurotic offered a precise symptom—which was not always the case—and its meaning was discovered, the symptom was then supposed to disappear; but, although he often obtained good results with his patients, Reich established that their condition did not necessarily improve when they were made aware of the reason for their symptoms. Freud had acknowledged this difficulty during a meeting of the Vienna Psychoanalytic Society, confirming that a symptom could remain even after its cause had been discovered. Freud's statement lead Reich to question the method of treatment itself and the neurotic personality. He argued that if the release of repressed instincts is not always sufficient to effect the cure, this must mean that one requirement of the cure has not been met, and he asked himself what was lacking. This question later brought him to develop his orgasm theory.

In December 1920, Freud sent Reich a young student to analyze. The boy suffered from obsessions and many physiological problems; in the course of his treatment he masturbated, obtaining satisfaction for the first time, and Reich was surprised to watch his patient's symptoms fade away within one week. This incident was repeated on several occasions, with the symptoms reappearing after a period of time, until the moment Reich brought into the open the guilt feelings the patient associated with masturbation. After nine months of analysis the patient was much better.

Reich proved less successful with another patient. From January 1921 until October 1923 he worked with a waiter who was utterly incapable of having an erection. After more than two years of laborious psychoanalysis, they discovered the event that had triggered the patient's impotence: at the age of two he had witnessed his mother in childbirth, and the sight of the bleeding hole between his mother's thighs had given him a terrific shock. However, the discovery of the initial trauma, and the realization that the patient suffered from a castration complex, had no effect on his physical state; he remained as calm, placid and full of goodwill as ever.

Reich read a paper on this case at the technical seminar, and his older colleagues congratulated him on having correctly lit upon the original trauma. However, Reich was not satisfied. He had explained the origin of the symptom (the absence of an erection), yet this latter had not disappeared; he knew something was wrong with his therapeutic technique but was unable to decide what it was. Since the patient was "well adapted to reality" and worked normally, no one could guess at his lack of emotionality.

Some years later Reich came to understand the type of character terrain in which these symptoms "grew."

In 1922 Reich obtained his medical degree. He continued his psychiatric training at the university clinic under the direction of Professor Wagner-Jauregg (the inventor of malaria therapy, which treatment consists of innoculating the protozoan that causes malaria into patients suffering from general paresis—the fourth stage of syphilis). Reich was particularly interested in schizophrenia, before which the psychiatrists of the day found themselves defenseless.

In May 1922 the Psychoanalytic Dispensary of Vienna opened, with Dr. Edward Hitschmann as its director. Reich became the first assistant upon its foundation and remained so until 1928 when he became assistant chief, a position he held until 1930.

The eight years he worked in this clinic were of great importance to Reich. Among other things he realized that neuroses were prolific at all levels of society, limiting the efficiency of psychoanalysis on a collective scale. A psychoanalytic treatment called for hundreds of sessions, each one lasting about one hour; and Reich saw that in order to cure all neurotics, one would need an army of psychoanalysts to dedicate themselves to treating the rest of the population—which was hardly a viable solution. He began to ask himself if it would not be better to invent methods of preventing neuroses. For this one would naturally have to alter the social condition of the people; but, as he relates, this approach was never considered by the other psychoanalysts:

Neither in psychiatry nor in psychoanalysis was it customary to ask patients about their *social conditions.* That there were poverty and need, one knew; but somehow that did not seem to be relevant. In the clinic, however, one was constantly confronted by these factors. Often enough, social help was the first thing necessary. Suddenly, the fundamental *difference between private practice and clinic practice* was evident. After some two years of clinic work it was clear that *individual psychotherapy has a very limited scope.* Only a small fraction of the psychically sick could receive any treatment.[4]

In September 1922, at the International Psychoanalytic Congress in Berlin, the presence of several Americans testified to the fact that Freud's ideas were meeting with larger and larger audiences. Among the subjects tackled was that of therapeutic techniques, a problem which was preoccupying Freud at the time. Technique lagged considerably behind the justifiably called "theory." The mechanics of the cure were not properly understood and an analysis could drag on for years without obtaining any appreciable results.

On returning to Vienna, Reich proposed to his younger colleagues that they found a psychoanalytic therapy seminar; Freud wholeheartedly approved of this initiative. From 1922 to 1924 the leadership of the seminar was entrusted first to Hitschmann and then to Nunberg. From 1924 to 1930 Reich took over its direction. It was in the course of this seminar that he elaborated the elements of his theory on the function of the orgasm and character analysis.

---

[4]*Ibid.,* p. 54.

Chapter II

The Psychoanalytic Theory of Neuroses

By the time Reich had begun to study psychoanalysis, much of Freud's basic thinking on the etiology of neuroses had been generally accepted by his colleagues (if not by the population as a whole). Reich's own controversial opinions on the function of the orgasm and character analysis were based on his knowledge of the Freudian theories and his experience with current therapeutic techniques, a summary of which follows.—[*Translator*].

1. Infant Sexuality

In making his most violently opposed disclosure concerning the existence of a sexual life in infants, Freud had broadened the notion of sexuality. It is no longer considered merely subordinate to procreation: it is a means of procuring pleasure; sexuality is in fact the function of pleasure. The infant is a small animal seeking pleasure by stimulating various parts of its body. In principle any part of the body can be a source of pleasure, but there are preferred zones, called *erogenous zones* by Freud, around which the sexual activity of the infant is concentrated. It is noteworthy that at this early stage sexual activity is not directed toward another person, which justifies the *autoerotic* qualification Freud gave it.

1.A. The Oral Phase

The first sexual manifestation of the infant is sucking, which appears during the first year. There is every reason to believe that while it is being nursed, the child learns to derive pleasure through the rhythmic contractions of the lips and tongue. Since the mouth plays the part of the erogenous zone, this first stage in the sexual development is called the oral phase.

1.B. Sadistic Anal Phase

During the second and third years, the child exploits the excitability of the mucous membrane of the bowel by withholding the contents of its intestines. The accumulation of the stools and defecation give him pleasurable sensations. The satisfaction that he obtains in this way is severely repressed by those who are bringing him up; their attempts to train him in personal hygiene cause the first serious conflicts between the child and his environment. He is expected to go to the lavatory at a fixed time and taught that his excrement is dirty and disgusting, all of which deprives him of an important source of pleasure. Little by little the child renounces the pleasure that he took in manipulating his bowel movements.

Given the role anal eroticism plays in the onset of sadism, this second stage of the sexual development is known as the sadistic anal phase.

1.C. The Phallic Stage (fourth and fifth years)

In little boys the penis becomes the dominant erogenous zone; in little girls it is the clitoris.

Masturbation, which is the means of obtaining sexual satisfaction during this stage, is a universal phenomenon. However, pediatric literature before Freud rarely mentioned cases of infant onanism. This blindness on the part of parents and educators is not accidental; Freudians say that it is the manifestation of an unconscious resistance in the face of an embarrassing reality. Since official morality had relegated sexuality to the function of reproduction, all sexual activity that had in mind a goal other than the meeting of the spermatozoa with an ovum was ignored or condemned as degenerate.

1.D. The Latency Period

This period stretches from the sixth year until puberty. Confronted by the demands of school and family discipline, the child represses his sexual desires and loses the memory of his earlier sexual behavior; this is called infantile amnesia.

Thus we see the "reaction formations[1] of morality, shame and disgust" set in (Freud).

2. The Oedipus Complex

During the phallic stage, infant sexuality loses its autoerotic quality and turns toward other people. For the little boy the first love object will be his mother. The little girl finds herself in a symmetrical position, fixing her sexual desires on her father.

Observation of children shows that the little male wishes to monopolize his mother, to have her all to

---

[1]Reaction formation is a way of overcoming an impulse by turning it into the opposite of what it is. It is a double defense; not only is the temptation banished from consciousness, but the opposite attitude is adopted.

himself, and, at the same time, exhibits more or less overt hostility to the father, his rival. If everything goes well, the boy settles this conflict by identifying with the paternal image. Furthermore, when the child is chastised for masturbating, the fear of castration will come to the surface (many parents openly threaten to cut off their son's penis if he continues to play with it), helping the little boy to give up the idea of possessing his mother.

Now Freud has established that all neurotics without exception failed in their attempts to detach themselves from their mother. The castration complex persists as long as they live, as well as their dependence on paternal authority. This is the reason why Freud considered the Oedipus complex to be the nucleus of all neuroses.

Today we cannot fully appreciate the hatred and incomprehension that Freud faced when he revealed his discovery of the Oedipus complex. There was an outcry when he established that little boys desire their mothers, and little girls their fathers; and for several years the Oedipus complex was the favorite target of the enemies of psychoanalysis.

The reason for this aggression is easily understandable; in unveiling the existence of incestuous tendencies in the heart of the family circle, Freud was throwing a searchlight on the very foundations of that sanctuary of bourgeois values—the family.

3. The Conflict Theory

The idea of conflict occupies a central position in psychoanalysis and psychology. We speak of conflict when two impulses clash in the same individual. Unconscious conflicts almost always lead to more or less complicated psychological elaborations in human beings. On the other hand, animal psychology, whose study is founded on solid experimental bases, shows us cases of conflicts in their "pure state." Although we cannot apply all the results achieved from experiments on animals to human psychology, we can at least draw some conclusions from them. The examples that follow have been borrowed from animal psychology. Their value is primarily of an intuitive nature.

3.A. The Desire–Desire Conflict

The animal is simultaneously attracted by two separate objects. The story of the donkey hesitating between water and oats illustrates this situation.

3.B. The Aversion–Aversion Conflict

The animal is simultaneously repulsed by two different poles. Let us consider a rat placed between two points both of which have given him an electric shock; at a certain distance the tendency to escape from one of the dangerous areas is compensated for by his fear of the other. If there is no physical possibility of his escaping by following a perpendicular line at right angles to the one joining the two points, he will remain stationary midway between the two. Thus, to maintain the conflict, the rat must be confined in an inescapable enclosure.

3.C. The Desire–Aversion Conflict

A third possibility for conflict exists—where the animal is at the same time both attracted and repelled by a given situation. This type actually makes up a pathogenic conflict, as the following experiment, conducted by Jules H. Masserman, shows:
    Some cats were trained to lift the cover from a

little feeding trough in order to find some morsels of salmon. After this pattern had been well established, a mechanism was attached which threw blasts of air into the cats' faces when they sought out their food. It was then established that the cats hid at a certain distance from the feeding trough and could even have let themselves die of hunger. The trough was therefore the object of two antagonistic impulses—hunger and fear (of the the blast of air).

This experiment demonstrates: 1) that the tendency to approach an area associated with reward (in this case, food) diminishes slowly with distance; and 2) that the fear engendered by punishment is most intense in the immediate proximity of the goal, but rapidly diminishes as the animal moves away.

The following diagram illustrates the situation.

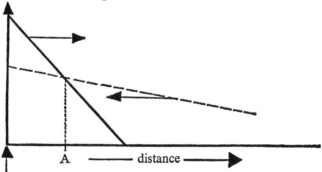

strength of the response

A   —— distance ——▶

but ambivalent

The broken line shows the tendency to escape from the ambivalent object; the dotted line indicates the tendency to approach. At point A the two impulses are equal. We see that when the animal is situated to the right of point A, the force that draws him toward his goal is stronger than the other. On the other hand, when he finds himself between the goal and point A, he is, as it were, repulsed. It follows that the animal will find himself immobilized at point A, which represents a state of stable equilibrium.[2]

Other experiments have ended with similar results. For example, a rat placed in a corridor at one end of which he has received food followed by electric shocks, runs a certain distance then stops.

Contrary to the aversion–aversion conflict, it is not necessary to imprison the animal to continue this conflict. Whatever his position, he will end up by finding himself immobilized on the spot where the two tendencies balance each other out.

As long as the conflict persists, the two tendencies involved will be maintained at a high level. The hunger (or sexual impulse if a sexual object is involved) is not satisfied, and the anxiety is not reduced. The effects of desire upon the animal can be observed through the agitation which does not cease until the desire has been satisfied. A prolonged conflict will upset all his behavior. The body adapts to face a stress situation—the heart beats faster, digestion is interrupted, and the organism is well prepared to face the danger. But a state of permanent anxiety has very detrimental consequences. (In this way, monkeys, rats and dogs have been given gastric ulcers.) Pavlov called the behavioral disorders that appear in animals which have been subjected to these experiments "experimental neuroses."[3]

---

[2]If the meaning of the two lines is reversed, that is to say, if the dotted line stands for repulsion and the broken line is attraction to the goal, A would stand for a state of unstable equilibrium. The slightest shift of this position would immediately lead the animal to move away.

[3]Arthur Koestler invented this example: If one trains a dog to run *behind* bicycles and to run *from* cars, then drives before him on a motorcycle, the dog will be subject to an experimental neurosis!

There is a relationship between experimental neuroses and human neuroses. When an individual's libido comes into conflict with forbidden social conduct embedded in the superego, conditions are ripe for the birth of character disorders. But the plasticity of the libido, which regresses toward infantile fixations, thus illuminating older conflicts, complicates the formation of the symptoms.

4. Human Neuroses

Freud distinguishes between "actual neuroses" and the appropriately named psychoneuroses.

4.1. Actual Neuroses

The actual neuroses group essentially covers neurasthenia and anxiety neuroses. These two disorders have a common etiology in that they are both caused by a current disturbance in the subject's sex life. Observation of neurasthenics has shown that their external symptoms (fatigue, headaches, back pains, etc.) come from excessive and unsatisfactory masturbation. The clinical picture of an anxiety neurosis is dominated by the anxiety attack (irregular heartbeats, palpitations, trembling, sweating, intolerable fear, and the sensation of suffocating, etc.). The chronic symptoms may persist in the intervals between the attacks. Anxiety neuroses on the other hand can be traced to prolonged abstinence or the repeated practice of coitus interruptus. In both cases, the libido turns into anxiety and finds release in this form. In the final analysis, it is then a lack of sexual satisfaction that determines the appearance of anxiety neuroses or neurasthenia.

It should be noted that in general one does not find any neurotic overtones accompanying these two disorders. The treatment consists of eliminating the harmful sexual practices without having recourse to the long analysis necessary for psychoneuroses.

4.2. Psychoneuroses

The mechanics of psychoneuroses are far more complicated than those of actual neuroses. Generally speaking, things happen as follows: the origin is found to be a conflict between the individual's genital needs and unconscious inhibitions. We saw in the preceding paragraphs that this type of conflict never resolves itself and that it has pathological effects on animals.

Since the libido is unable to find adequate release during the sexual act, this situation can trigger an anxiety neurosis. Jones, a disciple of Freud's, underlines this point in the following passage:

> There is an interesting clinical correlation between the actual neuroses and the psychoneuroses which is worthy of note. After a psychoneurotic structure has been demolished by means of psychoanalysis, one often finds, though not in the majority of cases, that a residual actual neurosis is left which had been, so to speak, the kernel of the whole disorder, and around which the psychogenetic symptoms had grouped themselves.[4]

(In anticipation of what is to follow, we should point out that Reich never tired of stressing this relationship because it allowed him to explain the source of energy which feeds psychoneurotic symptoms.)

Imprisoned by its conflict, the libido will under-

---

[4]Ernest Jones, *Papers on Psychoanalysis* (William Wood and Co.: New York, 1919), p. 394.

go an involution which Freud called *regression;* it will turn back to the earlier methods of satisfaction it found in the pregenital phases of its development.[5]

In short, when genital pleasure is obstructed, the sexuality turns toward the infantile stages that had earlier given the organism its sexual satisfaction. This regression is explained by the plasticity of the libido, and by the fact that the points of infantile fixation constitute permanent poles of attraction.

There is an alternative: either the individual adopts "aberrant" sexual behavior and becomes a "pervert," or the ego defends itself against these infantile sexual impulses, and we see a new conflict created which subtends the neurotic psychological elaborations. In an oft-quoted passage from his book *Three Essays on the Theory of Sexuality,* Freud summarizes this process:

> But psychoanalysis teaches us more than that. It shows that the symptoms do not by any means result at the expense only of the so-called normal sexual instinct (at least not exclusively or preponderately), but they represent the converted expression of impulses which in a broader sense might be designated as *perverse*

---

[5]It should be noted that the term regression in psychology has taken on a very general meaning; we speak of regression each time an individual reacts to a frustration by resorting to earlier objects or conduct.

For example, a child of seven, feeling the imminent birth of a brother or sister to be a threat to him, will become a baby himself once more.

Paul A. Osterrieth conducted an experiment that clearly demonstrates the mechanism of regression: One begins by ascertaining the apparent age of a certain number of children; then one allows them to play a game where the winners are rewarded (the losers are disappointed). One then reevaluates the apparent ages of the children and notices that the losers have regressed.

if they could manifest themselves directly in fantasies and acts without deviating from consciousness. The symptoms are, therefore, partially formed at the cost of abnormal sexuality. *The neurosis is, so to say, the negative of the perversion.*[6]

Let us note here that the regression can be toward a former stage of the sexual development, or toward the first sex objects (often the parent of the opposite sex).

If the libido has regressed to the infantile stages of its development, it revives partial tendencies which, if they are repressed, will creat a compulsion neurosis.

On the other hand, if the regression is toward the first sex objects, it creates incestuous tendencies whose repression causes hysteria. In this case, Oedipal fixations play the essential role in the formation of the symptoms.

In any case, psychoneurotic symptoms result from a compromise between the repressed impulses and the prohibition itself.

---

[6]*The Basic Writings of Sigmund Freud* (New York: Random House, 1938), pp. 574–575.

Chapter III

The Discovery of the Function of the Orgasm

Between 1920 and 1930, Reich became convinced that psychoneuroses stemmed from genital sexual disorders. The case of the two patients mentioned earlier had set him on the track. The first patient improved as soon as he became capable of experiencing genital satisfaction through masturbation; while the waiter hardly progressed at all, despite the reconstruction of the initial trauma.

By emphasizing the genital sexual role in the etiology of neuroses, Reich was developing an old idea of Freud's according to which all psychoneuroses grew round actual neuroses. In his *Introductory Lectures on Psychoanalysis,* Freud referred to it in these terms:

A noteworthy relation between the symptoms of the "actual" neuroses and of the psychoneuroses makes a further important contribution to our knowledge of the formation of symptoms in the latter. For a symptom of an "actual"

26

neurosis is often the nucleus and first stage of a psychoneurotic symptom.[1]

And in *The Function of the Orgasm* (p. 67), Reich wrote: "This illuminating statement, which Freud never followed up, was the starting point of my own investigations of stasis anxiety."

In stressing that psychoneurotic symptoms drew their energy from the damming up of the organism's libido because of a conflict with unconscious inhibitions, Reich's conception of psychoneuroses hardly differed from that of Freud who centered his treatment around this assumption. Reich accorded more importance to the breaking up of the inhibitions themselves than most psychoanalysts, who spent their time interpreting dreams and "slips" in the hope of discovering the significance of these symptoms.

Reich was putting the sexual genital role in the etiology of psychoneuroses back in the foreground again. As a result, he was already coming into conflict with his colleagues' reserve, for by 1923, psychoanalysis had begun to acquire "freedom of the city" as an official science. After the hostile silence that had greeted its birth, this was a relief; but the change in attitude was accompanied by a retreat from psychoanalysis' most audacious theses, particularly those concerning sexuality. And naturally Reich's suggestion that one always finds genital sexual disorders accompanying neuroses was given a cool reception by his colleagues. But this did not stop him from pursuing his line of thought, and in November 1923 he gave his first paper on the subject, "Genitality from the point of view of psychoanalytic prognosis and therapy."

---

[1] *The Complete Introductory Lectures on Psychoanalysis* (New York: W. W. Norton, 1966), p. 390.

While I was talking, I became increasingly aware of a chilling of the atmosphere of the meeting. I used to speak well, and thus far had always found my audience attentive. When I finished, there was an icy stillness in the room. After a pause, the discussion began. My assertion that the genital disturbance was an important, and perhaps the most important symptom of the neurosis, was erroneous, they said. Even worse, they said, was my contention that an evaluation of genitality provided prognostic and therapeutic criteria.[2]

This paper, which contained the first rough outline of Reich's theory on the function of the orgasm, met with some serious arguments from his colleagues: many neurotics were not impotent; or again, it was thought that a woman who was capable of having a clitoral orgasm was genitally healthy. Reich defended himself after a fashion, pointing out that there were many impotent neurotics, and that all the women he had treated were vaginally frigid. But, as he acknowledged himself, his replies were hardly convincing; for if his assumption were correct, all neurotics must suffer from genital sexual disturbances—that is to say from their behavior during coitus.

He then started to question his patients, men and women, in detail about their behavior during the sexual act. It may seem surprising today, but other psychoanalysts were loath to discuss this subject with their patients, and accepted vague statements like, "I made love with him (or her)," at face value.

Furthermore, psychoanalysts only recognized two forms of impotence in a man: a man was con-

---

[2]*The Function of the Orgasm*, p. 75.

sidered impotent if he was incapable of having an erection, or if he did not succeed in ejaculating. Correlatively, it was said that a man was potent when he was able to carry out the sexual act. He was still more potent if he was able to accomplish this more often than once a night. As we can see, this concept of masculine potency or impotency corresponded to the common view.

As he listened to his patients describe exactly what they did and how they felt during the sexual act, it did not take Reich long to discover that his concept was far too confining; he became convinced that they all suffered from serious genital disturbances. This was borne out in particular by men who boasted about their conquests, and the number of times they could "do it" in one night. As far as erection was concerned these men were very potent, but ejaculation brought them very little pleasure, and sometimes none at all.

Reich then analyzed the fantasies associated with the sexual act. He realized that for many men intercourse assumed a pathological significance—to prove their virility, to conquer or rape a woman, to make up for a feeling of inferiority. They wanted to prove how long they could maintain an erection, and wanted to be admired for their virility. As for the women, they were always somewhat reticent, or else they experienced anxiety and guilt, and those with masochistic tendencies had rape fantasies. In brief, all sorts of parasitic meanings clung to the sexual act. In addition, said Reich, in none of the patients was there any hint of involuntary behavior or loss of alertness during the sexual act. All of them remained lucid, and never gave themselves up entirely. This is what Reich called "orgastic impotency."

At first he thought he had brought to light a new symptom, common to all neuroses. But, reflecting on the meaning of the Freudian theory which attributes to sexual malfunctions the prime role in the etiology of neuroses, Reich realized that orgastic impotency—that is to say the incapacity to give oneself totally during orgasm—was not an effect of the neurosis but its ultimate cause. In effect, Freud is saying that neuroses are provoked by unappeased genital desire. When a man is impotent, in the popular sense of the word, or when a woman is frigid, their genital impulses are unsatisfied, which maintains their neuroses. But if the neurotics are capable of actual intercourse something must happen during the sexual act to interfere with the discharge of their excitation. Impotence, in the popular sense of the word, only represents one instance of an incapacity to obtain genital satisfaction. If this conclusion is not accepted, we are renouncing in one fell swoop the fundamental concepts of psychoanalysis, argues Reich; and therefore, it is legitimate, and in accordance with Freudian doctrine, to study the behavior of patients during the sexual act.

Looked at from the psychic angle, the orgasm represents a discharge of sexual excitation, that is to say it should normally produce a certain amount of pleasure. In the male, erective and ejaculative power are necessary but not sufficient conditions to orgastic potency.

On the other hand, the orgasm is a reflex, that is to say an involuntary neuromuscular response involving the spinal cord rather than the brain. The importance of the lower segments of the spinal cord to sexual response was recognized as early as 1863 by Eckhardt, who showed that genital reactions could be provoked in the mammals in his laboratory by the electrical stimulation of the spinal cord. Further observations of human subjects have confirmed this fact.

If the brain remains active, voluntary motor reactions run the risk of interfering with the orgastic reflex.[3]

By combining these physiological facts with the psychological conception of the orgasm—a sharp reduction of sexual tension—Reich elaborated the theory of orgastic potency, which is the master key to his work:

"The involuntary contractions of the organism and the complete discharge of excitation are the most important criteria of orgastic potency."

Reich drew a chart of the sexual act made up of two distinct phases. During the first phase when sexual tension is heightened little by little by the addition of isolated sensations,[4] the partners' movements are controlled. The second phase, that of the involuntary muscular contractions, should be accom-

---

[3]When animal reflexes are studied, the brain is first destroyed to eliminate these reactions.

[4]This process is familiar to physiologists. For example, the muscular contractions that we accomplish each time we move result from the summation of little elementary jolts, each one taking up where the other left off. The aggregate effect is a fusion of the jolts into the tetanic contraction. The isolated muscular contraction is an artifact of the laboratory.

Another example is supplied by synaptic transmission. Before a given neurone can transmit nerve impulses, a minimum number of nerve endings must stimulate it in an interval of approximately 0.2 seconds; this is called the period of "synaptic delay."

panied by a "more or less intense clouding of consciousness." The sexual tension built up during the preceding phase is released during the orgasm and leads the organism to a state of equilibrium bringing him a certain amount of pleasure. This pleasure is even more intense when the discharge of excitation is faster.

The clouding of consciousness and the involuntary muscle contractions are the two criteria by which we judge if an individual is orgastically potent.

Now Reich ascertained that all his patients, without exception, remained more or less lucid during the ultimate phase of the sexual act, they did not surrender to it entirely. He deduced from this that a certain quantity of energy remained dammed-up in the organism, and that this obstruction, which he called the *sexual stasis,* supplied the neurotic symptoms with an endless source of energy.

Some psychoanalysts wrongly interpreted the orgasm theory by advising their patients to have sexual intercourse. They had understood that a lack of sexual satisfaction provoked neuroses—which is true—but they overlooked the fact that the patients are incapable of deriving sufficient pleasure from the orgasm, because of the internal blockage, and because the libido is partly fixed on pregenital stages. Therefore the goal of a treatment should be to eliminate orgastic anxiety, and free the libido of its infantile attachments. For example, there are men to whom lovemaking means piercing or raping their partners; this shows sadistic tendencies caused by a former sexual frustration which arose at the age of four or five when the libido was in its phallic stage. To restore orgastic potency, one must begin by countering the infantile fixation, which will result in a strengthening of the genital impulses.

The orgasm theory and the idea of orgastic potency which is derived from it, opens up a far wider area than genital sexuality.

Prior to this, it was thought that a man who succeeded in penetrating a woman and ejaculating or a woman who derived pleasure from the stimulation of her clitoris, were generally healthy. As we have seen Reich felt that this was not sufficient.

In addition, the sexual stasis gives us a coherent explanation of the quantitative factor of actual neuroses and psychoneuroses. (Reich now substituted the term "stasis neurosis" for "actual neurosis.")

The sexual stasis is then the difference between the quantity of sexual energy stored up in the organism prior to orgasm, and the amount that is released during the orgasm. In an orgastically potent individual, these two quantities are equal, and there is no difference; there is no sexual stasis. On the other hand, there is always a certain sexual tension in the neurotic, even if it does not appear to be such. The undischarged sexual energy will feed the inhibition which is hindering orgastic pleasure and the awareness of genital impulses; this vicious circle, where the sexual stasis maintains the inhibition, which then adds to the sexual stasis, is the nucleus of the stasis neurosis inherent in all neurotic troubles.

In the light of this discovery, Reich amended the Freudian theory of psychoneurosis as follows:

Once an inhibition has created the sexual stasis, this in turn may easily increase the inhibition and reactivate infantile ideas which then take the place of normal ones. That is, infantile experiences which in themselves are in no way pathological, may, due to present-day inhibitions, become endowed with an excess of sexual energy. Once that has happened, they become urgent; being in conflict with adult psychic organisation, they have to be kept down by repression. Thus, the chronic psychoneurosis with its infantile sexual content, develops on the basis of sexual inhibition which is conditioned by present-day circumstances and is apparently "harmless" at the outset. This is the nature of Freud's "regression to infantile mechanisms." All cases that I have treated showed this mechanism. If the neurosis had developed not in childhood but at a later age, it was shown regularly that some "normal" inhibition or difficulty of the sexual life had created a stasis, and this in turn had reactivated infantile incestuous desires and sexual anxieties.[5]

Reich further continues:

The central psychic conflict is the sexual child-parent relationship. It is present in every neurosis. It is the *historical* experiential *material* that furnishes the *content* of the neurosis. All neurotic fantasies stem from the infantile sexual attachment to the parents. But the child-parent conflict could not produce an enduring disturbance of the psychic equilibrium if it were not continually nourished by the actual stasis which this conflict itself originally produced. Sexual stasis is, therefore, the etiological factor which

---

[5]*The Function of the Orgasm,* pp. 71–72.

—constantly present in the immediate situation —affords to the neurosis, not its content, but its *energy.* The historical pathological incestuous attachment to parents and siblings loses its strength when the energy stasis in the immediate situation is eliminated; in other words, when full orgastic gratification takes place in the immediate present. *The pathogenicity of the Oedipus complex,* therefore, depends on *whether or not there is a physiologically adequate discharge of sexual energy.* Thus, actual neurosis (stasis neurosis) and psychoneurosis are interwoven, and cannot be thought of as independent of each other.[6]

As we can see, Reich never questioned the existence of the mechanisms (libido regression, repression, etc.) that Freud had discovered. He limited himself to stating that the sexual stasis is the energy source of the neurosis. Psychoanalysis should have accepted Reich's discoveries on the function of the orgasm at first glance, and it would have benefited from them considerably—as Reich, of course, intended.

---

[6]*Ibid.,* pp. 89–90.

Chapter IV

Resistance Interpretation and Character Analysis

1. The Interpretation of Resistances

During the years 1922 to 1926 Reich's ideas matured and became more clearly defined as he gathered observations to support his theory on the function of the orgasm.

At the Psychoanalytic Congress in Salzburg in 1924, he explained to his colleagues what he understood by the term "orgastic potency" and maintained that all neuroses stem from disturbed genital sexuality. This being the case, Reich emphasized the need to restore the patient's orgastic potency. Reich's first break with orthodox psychoanalysis became apparent at this point, for in holding genital disorders principally responsible for all neuroses, he concluded that the task of the therapist must be to destroy the inhibitions which prevent complete genital satisfaction. To be sure, he had not yet formulated his ideas on how this should be carried out. But the discussions that took place at the Technical Seminar for Psychoanalytic Therapy centered more and more on the resistances put up by patients in the course of their treatment. Reich was concentrating his efforts on the analysis of these resistances and chose to delay his interpretation of the material which the patients "volunteered" (accounts of dreams, slips of the tongue, expressions, free associations, and so on). Without suspecting it, he was imperceptibly moving away from the classical modes of therapy.

The first real evidence to emerge from the exchanges between the members of the technical seminar (directed by Reich from 1924 to 1930) was that psychoanalysts were hesitant to encourage patients to express their aggression. They preferred to deal with likable and easygoing persons, as Reich wryly noted in *Character Analysis:*

> True, it may be more pleasant to treat a polite patient than an impolite, very candid one, who tells the analyst that he is too young or too old, that he has a shabby apartment or an ugly wife, that he looks stupid or too Jewish, that he behaves neurotically and better go for analysis himself.[1]

It is disagreeable for a doctor to have a patient who swiftly discovers the chinks in his armor; he could become defensive himself and run the risk of reacting more or less openly to the personal attacks his patient launches. Under these circumstances, the successful progress of the treatment, to say the least, is compromised.

---

[1] *Character Analysis* (New York: Farrar, Straus & Giroux, 1969), p. 30.

The psychoanalyst's reserve in the face of his patient's hostility results nine times out of ten in a process of mutual adjustment. The patient detects the doctor's coldness whenever he behaves aggressively and his tacit approval each time he complies with his wishes. These interactions between therapist and patient cause the patient to adopt only "cooperative" attitudes and to suppress the behavior that the analyst finds hard to tolerate.

One consequence of this state of affairs was that negative transference was seldom mentioned anymore. In psychoanalysis, as we know, the term "transference" refers to the affective attitudes that emerge and are oriented toward the analyst. These attitudes reproduce the feelings that the patient had for the people who surrounded him when he was a child and that rise to the surface of consciousness during his analysis. If the patient falls in love with his analyst, it is called positive transference; on the other hand, if he shows hostility or hatred it is called negative transference. The psychoanalysts were evading the latter because they felt challenged by their patients.

The development of a false positive transference masks hostile sentiments in the patient, who then leads his analyst into a series of cul-de-sacs by routinely accepting all his interpretations. In this way the psychoanalysts negate the effect of the well-known principle of "catharsis"—i.e., that the recollection of traumatic childhood experiences or the sudden release of repressed impulses contribute largely to the cure. For in the presence of a false positive transference, such consciousness may often remain cerebral and not be accompanied by any outward relief from the symptom. The patient agrees to the interpretation that his analyst suggests, but feels nothing at all. The discovery of repressions has not given rise to any emotional release and the benefit of it is lost.

Reich and his seminar colleagues learned to be suspicious of treatments that progressed too well. When the patients supplied abundant material which was relatively easy to interpret, the analysts wound up by discovering that the profusion of dreams and transparent symbols were masking an unsuspected resistance. Some patients, who were up to date with psychoanalytic theories, lost no time in juggling with the terminology; they referred to their "Oedipus complex" or their "infantile fixations" without any apparent effect. If they were astute, they discovered what the analyst was expecting of them and furnished him with splendid dreams and limpid associations. The analyst was delighted and swallowed every word they said, without realizing that he was allowing himself to be shunted into a backwater. Often patients reduced their analyst to blind rage by more or less deliberately putting him off the scent, and telling him such confused dreams that he could not hope to understand them.

On the other hand, said Reich, the majority of analyses were chaotic; the patients gave up their material in bulk, the treatment was conducted on a day-to-day basis without any order or method, and no real advance was made; if there was sporadic improvement, no one understood why. Most cases just fizzled out. Having observed some of these chaotic treatments, Reich arrived at the conclusion that he should first go to work systematically on the resistances.

He and his colleagues decided not to begin the interpretation of material until they had brought all their patients' ever-present resistances into the open. Thus they were drawing away from the classic modes of therapy which held that one should "always proceed from the surface," interpreting the material progressively as the patients presented it.

In June 1926, Reich read a paper at his seminar which added the final period to the subject. The first rule for resistance analysis, he said, is the following: "No interpretation of meaning should be made when a resistance interpretation is needed."

That is to say one must avoid working on the material coming from the deepest layers of the unconscious as long as one has not located and eliminated the superficial defense mechanisms. If the material is interpreted before the corresponding resistances are eliminated, the interpretation loses its therapeutic effectiveness, and the patient accepts or rejects this interpretation according to the transference situation. By analyzing the resistances as they present themselves, one avoids the chaotic situations which arise with the unsystematic interpretation of material. This often happens when the patient supplies abundant material coming from all layers of the unconscious and corresponding to all ages. The structure of the unconscious, said Reich, reminds one of the formation of the earth, where geologists can distinguish various strata, each of which has its own history and was formed during different eras. An analysis should proceed in an orderly fashion, cutting through the superficial zones —that is to say the most recent—in order to get at the oldest ones. If this method is not followed, little progress is made; the patient apparently produces very rich material, and the analyst proposes several interpretations that do not succeed in bringing about any effect. Finally, but usually too late, the analyst realizes that the patient has been going round in circles, constantly presenting the same material under different guises. The danger of these chaotic analyses, says Reich, is that the doctor continues to believe everything is going well, simply because the patient is "bringing material" when, in reality, he is slipping away.

Reich stressed the difficulty there is in discovering latent resistances as against clear-cut resistances when the patient continually arrives late, remains silent, or shows hostility toward his analyst. Latent resistances can be hidden behind the most eager cooperation, notably in the form of a total absence of reticence. In this case Reich wrote:

> I tackle such latent resistances as soon as I perceive them and do not hesitate to interrupt the patient's communications as soon as I have heard enough to understand the resistance. For experience shows that the therapeutic effect of the patient's communications is lost if they are made in the presence of unresolved resistances.[2]

Reich also deplored the tendency of underestimating the importance of the patient's behavior in the course of the sessions: his way of speaking, the expression on his face, how he uses his hands, etc. It is general practice, he says, to concentrate one's attention on what the patient is saying and ignore the way in which he is saying it. Yet the patient's attitudes are the gauge by which we can infer the eventual existence of a latent resistance.

---

[2]*Character Analysis,* p. 28.

Reich pointed out that neurotics have somehow achieved a certain psychological balance and consider their psychoanalysts' efforts to uncover their repressions to be a threat. The analysts' insistence on forcing the patients to face what they are attempting to escape from, leads the patients to build up their defenses against the repressed impulses. Since the analysts reactivate old conflicts by trying to dislodge the dangerous material, they become intruders and the patients project onto them the defenses built up against their (the patients') unconscious. And as the disturbers of neurotic balance, the analysts automatically become the enemy. Reich stressed that this process is achieved independently of the repressed impulses (love, hate, homosexual tendencies, and so on).

He concluded his statement by emphasizing the importance of completing the resistance analysis and being prepared to suspend the analysis of material for as long as necessary. Since this proposal differed from current therapy techniques, Reich had to face some criticism. What is more, the final goal of the treatment was to restore orgastic potency; and there were few psychoanalysts who shared this point of view. For several years Reich dealt tactfully with the dissenters by avoiding the expression of his ideas in too direct a form.

Freud was present in December 1926 when Reich gave a lecture on resistance analysis:

> As the central problem I presented the question as to whether, in the presence of a latent negative attitude, one should interpret the patient's incestuous desires, or whether one would have to wait until the patient's distrust was eliminated. Freud interrupted me: "Why would you

not interpret the material in the order in which it appears? *Of course* one has to analyze and interpret incest dreams as soon as they appear." This I had not expected. I kept on substantiating my point of view. The whole idea was foreign to Freud. He did not see why one should follow the line of the resistances instead of that of material. In private conversations about technique he seemed to have thought differently. The atmosphere of the meeting was unpleasant. My opponents in the seminar gloated and pitied me. I remained calm.[3]

2. Character Armor

Reich was intrigued by patients whose symptoms disappeared during psychoanalytic treatment but who still did not obtain full genital satisfaction from an orgasm. In this case he maintained that a sexual stasis must persist, yet since there were no neurotic symptoms he asked himself how this observation could be reconciled with the orgasm theory.

Admittedly the libido has been shaped by pregenital symptoms and fixations and yet the destruction of the neurotic formations did not always have the anticipated results, that is, the restoration of the orgasmic reflex. The patients effectively got rid of their symptoms, and the neurosis lost its more striking characteristics, but orgastic impotence continued. Reich and his colleagues should have anticipated that the residual sexual stasis would bring on a fit of anxiety, as in anxiety neuroses, but they saw no similarity. This problem led Reich to ask himself a question which proved fruitful—"Besides the neurotic symptoms, where does sexual energy find its release?"

[3]*The Function of the Orgasm,* p. 142.

We have seen that the analysis of resistances was an indispensable preliminary to the interpretation of material. By isolating an ego defense, the unconscious element against which this defense had been built up was liberated not only intellectually (the patient becoming conscious of it) but affectively (the patient experiencing this consciousness, and feeling it emotionally).

As Reich perfected his therapeutic technique, experience taught him that a whole series of resistances can be observed in the patients' behavior—in their way of remaining silent, of talking, of walking, of looking at the analyst, etc. This discovery led him to introduce an aspect that psychoanalysis had never really taken into account, that of the patient's character. (It is true that Adler found character very important, but he had abandoned all references to sexuality in explaining neuroses and was no longer part of the psychoanalytic movement.)

Reich could not understand why his older colleagues neglected to analyze the patient's behavior, yet never hesitated to infer a chain of unconscious mental processes from slips of the tongue. Could the way in which a patient behaves during his session be less significant than some slip, he argued. For example, when a patient speaks about his mother, the tone in which he expresses himself is perhaps more revealing of his feelings in regard to his mother than what he is actually saying.

The character, which determines the subject's way of being, is made up of a web of unconscious defenses which repress impulses that society frowns upon (aggression, and the like) and which insulate the individual from the outside world.

For example, excessive politeness betrays a reaction against sadistic tendencies. The character has formed an armor which protects the subject against stimuli from the outside world and from his own unconscious. In analyzing the role of this armor, Reich arrived at the conclusion that it fulfilled an economic function: that of absorbing anxiety stemming from the sexual stasis. In effect, anxiety and sadistic impulses stemming from sexual frustration create reaction neuroses and give rise to more or less pathological compensations. Instead of expressing itself in obsessive symptoms (a tic, for example), anxiety can form part of the character armor and shows in the neurotic character traits. For example, there are people who are never certain that they have turned off the gas before leaving home; if they have to go back upstairs four times before they have a clear conscience, they are exhibiting obsessive symptoms expressing an unconscious anxiety. But anxiety can also manifest itself indirectly in character traits which are less obvious than the above symptoms. This replies to the question asked earlier, where Reich admitted to being disconcerted by the absence of anxiety and neurotic symptoms in orgastically impotent individuals. He asked himself what happened to the unreleased sexual energy; normally it would be released in the form of an anxiety neurosis or hidden behind the symptoms. In fact, it can serve to cement the neurotic character:

> *Economically* speaking, the character in ordinary life and the character resistance in the analysis serve the same function, that of avoiding unpleasure, of establishing and maintaining a psychic equilibrium—neurotic though it may be—and finally, that of absorbing repressed

energies. One of its cardinal functions is that of binding "free floating anxiety," or, in other words, that of absorbing dammed-up energy.[4]

Some pyschoanalysts made a distinction between "character" neuroses and "symptom" neuroses. Reich denounced this distinction, asserting that all neurotics have neurotic characters which may or may not have visible symptoms. The only difference between character neuroses and symptom neuroses is that, in the case of the latter, the neurotic character produced the symptom. Since symptom neuroses always have a neurotic character base, character resistances will reveal themselves in the course of the treatment. He concluded that all analyses should therefore go through a character analytic stage.

Character neuroses can be first recognized by the fact that the patient does not feel particularly sick. The symptom is looked upon as a foreign body, a sort of cyst in the personality which can poison the life of the neurotic. In character neuroses, the patient does not exhibit actual symptoms, but neurotic character traits which he cannot recognize as such. When he is confronted with one of his symptoms, the patient defends himself by inventing all sorts of rationalizations. On the other hand, a patient suffering from agoraphobia or impotence does not resort to these subterfuges.

What is more, a symptom may be dissimulated by a character neurotic. For example, the act of washing the hands thirty times a day could be attributed to a mania for order and meticulousness

---

[4]*Character Analysis*, p. 48.

and not appear particularly out of place to the neurotic patient or his family. As we can see, the demarcation line between neurotic symptoms and pathological character traits is quite fluid. Reich had observed in his patients all the nuances between the symptom and the neurosis.

In view of the preceding discoveries it must be borne in mind that the symptoms could not have developed without a neurotic characterological basis; that this is shown in the general behavior of the patient; and that it was formed during the first years of the patient's life. The character represents the way an individual differs from other people and is the total expression of his whole past. While a symptom can emerge quickly, character traits take years to build up, and are not as easy to isolate as symptoms.

Reich, then, had discovered a pathological character structure in his patients that the individual had built up bit by bit in earliest infancy, while attempting to adapt to the demands of his surroundings. This character structure constantly minimizes anxiety and automatically filters the internal and external stimuli which could disturb the subject. The neurotic has formed character armor that imprisons him in a net of rigid and stereotyped reactions, making him impervious to certain logical reasoning and anything that could cast a doubt on the compromises he has made between his impulses and his social obligations. In the course of treatment, psychoanalysts come up against this barrier because the patient defends himself against everything that threatens his neurotic balance:

The totality of the neurotic character traits makes itself felt in the analysis as a compact defense mechanism against our therapeutic endeavors . . . During analysis, the character of a patient soon becomes a resistance. That is, in ordinary life, the character plays the same role as in analysis: that of a psychic protection mechanism. The individual is "characterologically armored" against the outer world and against his unconscious drives.[5]

A few years later, while he was studying the irrational behavior of the masses, Reich saw evidence of the neurotic character on a collective scale. A population composed of frustrated individuals, who repress their hostility, behaves in a pathological manner and demonstrates that it is inaccessible to logical reasoning; which partly explains the success of demagogic propaganda and the failure of most attempts to arouse a revolutionary spirit in the heart of the masses.

3. Character Analysis

We have seen that there is no inherent difference between neurotic character traits and so-called symptoms. A symptom appears like an island in the middle of the ocean. There is no way of rationalizing it, while a neurotic character trait must be continually emphasized so that the patient adopts the same attitude toward it as he does toward the symptom.

In order to release these pathological character traits, the analyst will commence the treatment by dissecting the patient's character. This proceeding prolongs the resistance analysis technique by pay-

[5]*Character Analysis,* pp. 44, 48.

ing special attention to those resistances which show up in the patient's attitudes:

> In character analysis, we ask ourselves *why* the patient deceives, talks in a confused manner, why he is affect-blocked, etc.; we try to arouse the patient's interest in his character traits in order to be able, with his help, to explore analytically their origin and meaning. All we do is to lift the character trait which presents the cardinal resistance out of the level of the personality and show to the patient, if possible, the superficial connections between character and symptoms. . . . In principle, the procedure is not different from the analysis of a symptom. What is added in character analysis is merely that we isolate the character trait and confront the patient with it repeatedly until he begins to look at it objectively and to experience it like a painful symptom; thus, the character trait begins to be experienced as a foreign body which the patient wants to get rid of.[6]

Reich illustrates this method by describing several cases. He cites the example of a man who had a passive, feminine nature, and suffered from premature ejaculation. As Reich progressively threw his passiveness and submission into relief, the patient tended to become hostile, because his femininity was a reaction to his hostile tendencies. In uncovering the repressed aggression, Reich discovered an infantile castration anxiety which had earlier caused the patient to dissimulate his hatred of his father through apparent submission. In this way, starting off with a character trait, Reich had gone right back to the Oedipus complex. In character analysis, then,

---

[6]*Character Analysis,* p. 50.

the psychoanalyst starts off with the most obvious resistances in the patient's general behavior and goes all the way back to forgotten infantile experiences. Once these have been exhumed, it becomes possible to understand the genesis of the neurotic character traits and to deal with them exactly as if they were symptoms. This approach means that one is constantly passing from the resistances to the material, but always giving preference to the resistance analysis at the start of the treatment. In the beginning, said Reich, the patient must be shown that he is resisting something; when he has recognized this, the infantile material, which helps one eliminate the resistances, is not slow in coming to the surface.

> If we put so much emphasis on the analysis of the *mode* of behavior, this does not imply a neglect of the contents. We only add something that hitherto has been neglected. Experience shows that the analysis of character resistances has to assume first rank. This does not mean, of course, that one would only analyze character resistances up to a certain date and then begin with the interpretation of contents. The two phases—resistance analysis and analysis of early infantile experiences—overlap essentially; only in the beginning, we have a preponderance of character analysis, that is, "education to analysis *by* analysis," while in the later stages the emphasis is on the contents and the infantile.[7]

The character analysis technique is in accordance with Freudian theories on the formation and dissolution of resistances, according to which a re-

---

[7]*Character Analysis,* pp. 51–52.

sistance is made up of a repressed impulse from the id, and another impulse from the ego repressing the first. These two impulses are unconscious, that is to say, the subject is not aware that he is repressing something. Reich confirms, then, that one must begin by making the ego defense conscious before going on to the analysis of the repressed impulse. Freud had not given any directions on this subject. In principle, it appeared that one could choose between the one or the other. For example, if a patient remains obstinately silent, the silence reflects a resistance against something. Let us suppose that the analyst is certain that it stems from a homosexual tendency. He can then directly tackle this tendency by informing the patient of its existence. But, Reich maintains this technique is inadvisable. It is better to first approach the ego defense, which is closer to the surface of consciousness. The patient is told he is remaining silent because the analysis has reached a critical stage. Without allusion being made to the homosexual impulse, he will be shown he is resisting something. And it is up to him to discover the nature of his fears. In order to do this, he must first realize that he is defending himself against an obscure facet of his personality.

The Freudian schema of the psychic apparatus consists of three compartments: the id, the superego, and the ego. The id and the superego are unconscious. The id forms a reservoir of repressed sexual impulses, and the superego consists of the barriers which dam up these impulses. The ego coincides with what we call consciousness. Following this schema, which only represents a rough approximation of reality, the aim of a treatment is to render the repressed instincts conscious. Freud sums it up in a concise formula, saying that "the ego should replace the id." Part of Reich's original contribution to psychoanalysis was to introduce another dimension to this psychic personality plan by adding the character; and in addition he improved therapeutic techniques by dislodging the resistances which protect the ego in order to get at the impulses buried in the id. According to Reich, one must not skirt around the defenses built up by the ego against repressed desires; on the contrary, one should start off with these resistances—which can be seen in the patient's attitudes—to disclose the forbidden material.

Reich worked five years, from 1922 to 1927, to perfect this technique. In his book *Character Analysis,* instead of losing himself in theoretical digressions or in involved explanations, he gives a series of practical and concrete instructions to enable the psychoanalysts to relate his techniques to their work. It was published in 1933 and met with great success among young German psychoanalysts who agreed to recognize the value of Reich's contribution to psychotherapy. Today character analysis is practiced by many American analysts; it is the only one of Reich's works to survive the progression of the psychoanalytic movement; the orgasm theory has been banished to the dungeon. But as Theodore P. Wolfe, Reich's American translator, has pointed out, one cannot accept the method of character analysis and ignore the orgasm theory as some practitioners have done. The aim of a character analysis, in effect, is to reestablish the orgastic reflex; the practice of character analysis and the orgasm theory are therefore inseparable.

Chapter V

The Contradictions of Psychoanalysis

I

One conclusion that could be drawn from the orgasm theory is that the awareness of genital impulses is not enough to produce a cure. It is necessary that these impulses be consummated. To put it another way, Reich established that the liberation of genital needs must be accompanied by their satisfaction; if these two conditions are not fulfilled simultaneously, the individual will remain or will become neurotic.

This assertion raises many problems, mainly because of the social norms which dictate that adolescents remain continent until their marriage. Marriage, puberty, and the social repression of sexual impulses quite naturally came up for discussion in the course of the seminar, but questions of this kind remained unasked outside the seminar. Reich sensed that he was going against the stream, and he was careful to avoid a head-on confrontation with his older colleagues:

> The actual goal of therapy, that of making the patient capable of orgasm, was not mentioned

in these first years of the seminar. I avoided the subject instinctively. It was not liked and aroused animosity.[1]

A little incident reveals the degree to which the orgasm theory was unpopular. Reich had put together his discoveries in a book *Die Funktion des Orgasmus*[2], in which he described his conception of the etiology of neuroses, the theory of orgastic potency and impotency, the sexual stasis, etc. On Freud's seventieth birthday, May 6, 1926, Reich presented him with the manuscript:

His reaction on reading the title was not gratifying. He looked at the manuscript, hesitated for a moment, and said, as if disturbed: "That thick?" I felt uneasy. That was not a rational reaction. He was always very polite and would not have made such a cutting remark without a basis. It had always been Freud's habit to read a manuscript in a few days and then give his opinion in writing. This time more than two months elapsed before I received his letter.[3]

---

[1] *The Function of the Orgasm*, p. 98.

[2] *Die Funktion des Orgasmus*, published in 1927 by the International Psychoanalytic Publishing House has little in common with *The Function of the Orgasm*, from which I have extracted several passages. *The Function of the Orgasm* is translated into English and is, in effect, Reich's autobiography, which he wrote in exile and which was first published in the United States in 1942.

Die Funktion des Orgasmus is a difficult and dense book, full of theoretical references, diagrams, and case histories presenting the orgasm theory scientifically.

Although these two books, *Die Funktion des Orgasmus* and *The Function of the Orgasm* have the same title, they differ greatly from each other.

[3] *Ibid.*, pp. 140–141.

II

The deep cause of the disagreement between Reich and Freud can be traced to the social implications of the orgasm theory. Reich maintained that it is "the lack of total and repeated sexual satisfaction" which causes neuroses. The idea that civilization would flounder in chaos if people "gave free rein to their instincts" is deeply rooted in morality, philosophy, and common belief. Freud shared this point of view. He always felt that "civilization" owed its existence to sexual repression, as he expressed on several occasions in his works. In the first chapter of *Introductory Lectures on Psychoanalysis,* Freud reviews the reasons why psychoanalysis was so beleaguered; showing that the social structure (which he refers to as "civilization") depends on sexual repression, and that all investigations into sexual realities come up against the existing hypocrisy:

> In my experience antipathy to this outcome of psychoanalytic research is the most important source of resistance which it has met with. Would you like to hear how we explain that fact? We believe that civilization has been created under the pressure of the exigencies of life at the cost of satisfaction of the instincts; and we believe that civilization is to a large extent being constantly created anew, since each individual who makes a fresh entry into human society repeats this sacrifice of instinctual satisfaction for the benefit of the whole community. Among the instinctual forces which are put to this use the sexual impulses play an important

part; in this process they are sublimated—that is to say, they are diverted from their sexual aims and directed to others that are socially higher and no longer sexual. But this arrangement is unstable; the sexual instincts are imperfectly tamed, and, in the case of every individual, who is supposed to join in the work of civilization, there is a risk that his sexual instincts may refuse to be put to that use. Society believes that no greater threat to its civilization could arise than if the sexual instincts were to be liberated and returned to their original aims. For this reason society does not wish to be reminded of this precarious portion of its foundations. It has no interest in the recognition of the strength of the sexual instincts or in the demonstration of the importance of sexual life to the individual. On the contrary, with an educational aim in view, it has set about diverting attention from that whole field of ideas. That is why it will not tolerate this outcome of psychoanalytic research and far prefers to stamp it as something aesthetically repulsive and morally reprehensible, or as something dangerous.[4]

On the other hand, experience had convinced Freud of the part played by sexual frustration in the etiology of neuroses. In particular, he had remarked that the repression of sexual behavior in the infant causes splits in his personality which will make hm vulnerable to nervous disorders in adulthood.

This is the fundamental contradiction which has plagued all Freudian thought. On the one hand, Freud felt sure that civilization was paying for its

---

[4]*The Complete Introductory Lectures on Psychoanalysis* (New York: W. W. Norton, 1966), pp. 22–23.

gains by sacrificing sexual satisfaction, but on the other hand, he stated that this sacrifice was causing deep psychological disturbances.

Freud was aware of this dilemma, which he sums up in these lines:

> What can we do when we are faced with infant sexual activity. We know the dangers we incur in smothering it, yet we do not dare to allow it to flourish unimpeded. The peoples of primitive societies and the lower classes in civilized society appear to allow their children complete sexual freedom. Without doubt they are thus building up an efficient protection against ulterior individual neuroses, but at what cost to civilization. One feels here that one is caught between Scylla and Charybdis.[5]

If Freud is right, the contradiction is not found in the thought, but is part of the human condition—like death. On the other hand, if he is wrong, that is to say, if sexual repression is not an inevitable consequence of civilization, we should reexamine the social causes for this repression.

Freud had been marked by his times and by his background (Austrian middle class at the end of the nineteenth century). He stayed away from political arguments and was not interested in social questions. His lack of sociological orientation together with his fairly conformist political opinions hardly disposed him to question the causes of sexual repression. Neither his courage nor his intellectual honesty were at fault, but the bourgeois horizons which always limited his philosophical and political perspectives.

---

[5]Translated from *Ma Vie et la Psychanalyse,* p. 178.

He postulated the existence of a special process, *sublimation,* which justified, to a certain extent, the repression of sexual instincts, and which toned down the pathogenic consequences of this repression:

> Among the factors which pit a so-called prophylactic act against a harmful act of privation, one has acquired particular social importance. It concerns the sexual tendency, which, having renounced partial pleasure of the act of procreation, has been replaced by another goal with a genetic relationship to the first, but which has stopped being sexual in order to become social. We give this process the name "sublimation," and in doing so we align ourselves with the general public which accords a greater value to social goals than sexual goals, for the latter are basically selfish goals. [Freud.]

For Freud, "civilization" (i.e., artistic works, telecommunications, the industrial infrastructure of modern societies, consumer goods, etc.) is built by abstract individuals who channel their sexual energy into their work. This view completely overlooks the concrete forms of the social systems through which civilization develops; it ignores the conditions of the working classes and does not take into account the fact that only a minority of people are able to "sublimate" their sexual needs, while others become neurotics whose work capacity diminishes. In addition, the Freudian theory of civilization reduces the whole of society to one individual. In order to comply with the demands of civilization, the individual must repress or sublimate his sexuality. Reich tells us that an eminent Hungarian psychoanalyst (probably Ferenczi) explained to him one day that the proletariat could be compared to the unconscious, because it indulged in unrepressed sexual practices. The bourgeoisie, however, corresponded to the ego and the superego, damming up the tumultuous forces of the unconscious.

III

The first problem that confronted Freud concerned the fate of the genital impulses liberated in the course of a treatment. Freud argued that the individual must sublimate his sexuality; that voluntary control must take the place of unconscious repression. Since civilization is based on the renunciation of sexual instincts, the individual cannot be allowed to exercise his genital sexuality unrestrainedly.

Reich, who was sure that psychological balance required a healthy sex life, could not accept the Freudian thesis which contradicted this evidence. He offered the example of a young hysterical girl who was made conscious, during a psychoanalytic session, of the incestuous character of her sexual desires. This awareness actually rid her of the incestuous tendencies, and her hysterical outbursts disappeared. But if the patient had successfully liquidated her Oedipus complex, she had not gone so far as to overcome her normal sexual desires. Reich maintains, quite obviously, that if a definitive cure is to be effected, these desires, hitherto associated with the paternal image, must be transferred to a lover and must be satisfied.

In any case, the new Freudian formulations made psychoanalysis less threatening to its enemies. The constant pressure brought to bear on the psychoanalytic movement by hostile forces contributed in large part to its degeneration.

This substitution of renunciation and rejection for repression seems to banish the ghost which raised its threatening head when Freud confronted the world with his early findings. These findings showed unequivocally that sexual repression makes people not only sick but also incapable of work and cultural achievement. The whole world began to rage against Freud because of the threat to morals and ethics, and reproached Freud with preaching the "living out," with threatening culture, etc. Freud's alleged antimoralism was one of the most potent weapons of his early opponents. This ghost did not begin to vanish until the theory of rejection was propounded; Freud's early assurance that he was affirming "culture," that his discoveries constituted no threat to it, had made little impression. This was shown by the never-ending talk about "pansexualism." Then, after the new formulation of rejection, the previous enmity was replaced by partial acceptance. For just as long as the instincts were not let out, it did not make any difference, from a "cultural point of view," whether it was the mechanism of instinctual rejection or that of repression which played the role of Cerberus keeping the shades of the underworld from emerging to the surface. One was even able to register progress: that from the unconscious repression of evil to the voluntary renunciation of instinctual gratification. Since ethics does not consist of being asexual but, on the contrary, in resisting sexual temptation, everybody can now agree with everybody.[6]

---

[6]*The Sexual Revolution* (Orgone Institute Press, 1945), p. 13.

IV

Dalbiez, the author of a book on psychoanalytic doctrine, wrote that Freud's work is a most lucid analysis of what is least human in human nature. If the expression "human nature" is not taken too literally, the remark is correct; psychoanalysts watch a stream of people passing through their offices—people who hate their children, who dream of eating excrement, or of violating corpses.

Those who are obliged to remain in daily contact with realities as disagreeable as these can easily become pessimistic about everything concerning the human animal. And if they do not constantly bear in mind that the individual is the product of his environment, they are tempted to consider the selfishness, pettiness, greed, or cruelty which people exhibit in their everyday life to be inherent in human nature.

Freud had a rather gloomy view of human nature; witness the following passage from *Civilization and Its Discontents:*

> Men are not gentle creatures who want to be loved, and who at the last can defend themselves if they are attacked; they are, on the contrary, creatures among whose instinctual endowments is to be reckoned a powerful share of aggressiveness. As a result, their neighbor is for them not only a potential helper or sexual object, but also someone who tempts them to satisfy their aggressiveness on him, to exploit his capacity for work without compensation, to use him sexually without his consent, to seize his possessions, to humiliate him, to cause him pain, to torture and to kill him. *Homo homini*

lupus. Who, in the face of all his experience of life and of history, will have the courage to dispute this assertion?

Freud was a liberal bourgeois who believed in progress and felt that with each generation man improved as he learned to master his egotistic tendencies. His lack of sociological training inclined him to believe that asocial behavior reflected inherent evil instincts. The unleashing of hatred and violence in the 1914–18 war, made a painful impression on him and confirmed his belief that harmful innate tendencies exist in man. In an article written during the war, Freud declared himself to be deeply affected by the acts of cruelty which marked the development of hostilities:

> But the war in which we did not want to believe broke out and brought . . . disappointments. It is not only bloodier and more destructive than any foregoing war, as a result of the tremendous development of weapons to attack and advance, but it is at least as cruel, bitter, and merciless as any earlier war. It places itself above all the restrictions pledged in times of peace, the so-called rights of nations; it does not acknowledge the prerogatives of the wounded and of physicians, the distinction between peaceful and fighting members of the population, or the claims of private property. It hurls down in blind rage whatever bars its way, as though there were to be no future and no peace after its effort. It tears asunder all community bonds among the struggling peoples and threatens to leave bitterness which will make impossible any re-establishment of these ties for a long time.[7]

[7]*Reflections on War and Death* (Moffat, Yard & Co., 1918), pp. 11–12.

As Freud testified, the disappointment he suffered made him lose the illusions he was nourishing about the degree of civilization attained by Europeans.

He then questioned himself about the process by which the socialization of individuals was accomplished. According to him, mankind's genetic heritage is made up of evil tendencies which the individual finally gives up under the pressure of education:

> In reality, there is no such thing as "eradicating" evil. Psychological, or strictly speaking psychoanalytic investigation proves, on the contrary, that the deepest character of man consists of impulses of an elemental kind which are similar in all human beings, the aim of which is the gratification of certain primitive needs.[8]

To a pessimistic mind imprisoned by bourgeois values and with little sociological training, the frequency of aggressive and destructive behavior in man must inevitably suggest that hereditary instincts exist to maintain these attitudes.

Freud then published two essays in which he attempted to justify this view. The first appeared in 1920 and was titled *Beyond the Pleasure Principle*. The second was published three years later, under the title *The Ego and the Id*.

In these two works, Freud got bogged down in pseudo-scientific explanations as he attempted to prove that a "death instinct" exists in all human beings which accounts for their destructive behavior. Although he used biological arguments to justify the existence of this instinct, the way in which he went

---

[8]*Ibid.*, p. 18.

about it must not be allowed to deceive the reader; the death instinct is merely a rationalization of the attitude that man is naturally violent, aggressive, and dangerous to his fellow creatures.

V

In *Beyond the Pleasure Principle,* Freud formulated the theory of the "compulsion to repeat," which may be observed, according to him, in numerous human activities. For example, children like to hear again a story that they have enjoyed or to play enjoyable games over and over again, etc. This compulsion to repeat, Freud maintains, is a phenomenon which cannot be defined by any psychological explanation. It can cause individuals to repeat the same mistakes, harmful experiences, and failures. When this compulsion to repeat stands in the way of the *pleasure principle,* Freud sees something "demonical" about it. Human behavior, he maintains, is governed by the pleasure principle: that which procures pleasure attracts, that which produces displeasure repels. The fact that the compulsion to repeat can hinder the pleasure principle led Freud to ask himself whether it is the key to a very deep instinctive tendency:

But how is the predicate of being "instinctual" related to the compulsion to repeat? At this point we cannot escape the suspicion that we may have come upon the track of a universal attribute of instincts and perhaps of organic life in general which has not hitherto been clearly recognized or at least not explicitly stressed. It seems, then, that an instinct is an urge inherent in organic life to restore an earlier state of things which the living entity has been obliged to abandon under the pressure of external disturbing forces; that is, it is a kind of organic elasticity, or, to put it another way, the expression of the inertia inherent in organic life.[9]

Freud had therefore developed the theory that an instinct is in fact the tendency to reduce the organism to a former state. Pushing his reasoning to its limits, he arrived at the conclusion that an instinct exists to lead living beings to return to the state of inanimate matter, since this state preceded the appearance of life on earth.

He suggests that this "death instinct" is at work in the heart of all living cells, although the sexual instinct (which Freud called "Eros" from then on) could mask its existence. Living beings are the seat of a struggle between the death instinct (Thanatos) which aims to make them fall back into nothingness, and the life instinct (Eros) which is trying to keep them alive.

Freud was attracted by the idea that Thanatos always won. He reviewed many arguments both in support of, and in opposition to, his hypothesis. He mentioned the experiments of an American biologist who had cultivated protozoa by isolating at each mitosis one of the two daughter nuclei. After a great many mitosic divisions, the last generation cell was as fresh as the protozoan at the start, which seemed to prove the potential immortality of unicellular animals. Freud then cites other experiments which had ended with the opposite result and points out that this contradiction in the results is due to the fact that the first biologist placed each new mitosic cell in a fresh nutrient solution; if, on the

---

[9]*Beyond the Pleasure Principle,* Standard Edition of the Complete Psychological Works, vol. 18, p. 36.

other hand, one leaves a microbic culture to itself, it will die in the end because of the saturation of the environment by the wastes of metabolism. Thus, Freud concludes, death can be artificially deferred by laboratory process, but it intervenes normally under ordinary conditions even in unicellular organisms. Next he examined to what extent the famous Weismann theory on the segregation of germ cells from the soma could support his hypothesis on the dual character of human nature; he says, in passing, that catabolism (that is to say, all the biochemical reactions of organic breaking down) could very well constitute the biological basis of the death instinct, while the life instinct is rooted in anabolism (that is, all biochemical reactions to organic synthesis), etc.

The reticence with which Freud advanced these speculations is extremely curious. He took care to say that he himself did not attribute much importance to them, that he was simply letting his imagination wander. One has the impression that he was aware of venturing upon slippery ground. The following passage betrays his hesitations:

> It may be asked whether and how far I am myself convinced of the truth of the hypotheses that have been set out in these pages. My answer would be that I am not convinced myself and that I do not seek to persuade other people to believe in them. Or, more precisely, that I do not know how far I believe in them. There is no reason, as it seems to me, why the emotional factor of conviction should enter into this question at all. It is possible to throw oneself into a line of thought and to follow it wherever it leads out of simple scientific curiosity, or, if the

reader prefers, as an *advocatus diaboli,* who has not sold himself to the devil.[10]

A little further on, Freud recognizes that he allowed himself to be led far from the facts.

Three years later Freud published *The Ego and the Id.* The tone is much more positive than it was in *Beyond the Pleasure Principle.* From now on he takes it for granted that there are two groups of instincts at work in the heart of all living matter. In the human being, he maintains, these instincts become confused, which allowed him to explain the sadistic or masochistic tendencies that can be observed in the sexual behavior of certain persons.

In an earlier work Freud had introduced the notion of the superego. He elaborated this theory here, explaining that the superego results from the interiorization of the constraints that the individual has experienced in the course of his life. By identifying himself with the image of the parent who caused him the most frustration, the infant liquidates his Oedipus conflict, which caused Freud to remark that the superego is heir to the Oedipus complex.

The emphasis placed on the superego shifted the interest that psychoanalysts had hitherto shown in the sexual impulses to more ethereal regions.

Until now, it had been thought that neuroses resulted from a conflict between the sexual instinct and society. This concept implied criticism of the moral code and of sexual repression. But Freud and the psychoanalysts were now according more and more importance to the conflicts between the ego and the superego and progressively abandoning the old idea that lack of sexual satisfaction provokes

---

[10]*Ibid.,* p. 59.

neuroses. Instead of speaking of a conflict between sexuality and the demands of society interiorized by the superego, they preferred to say that the neuroses stemmed from a conflict between the ego and the superego. People no longer fell sick because of the repression of their sexuality; they were being tyrannized by their superego.

In this regard, Freud developed the idea that the superego could become a reservoir where all the destructive impulses were accumulated. By observing the relentlessness with which many of his patients clung to their neuroses, he inferred that they felt the need to remain sick rather than be cured. He reasoned that this was because they suffered from very deep guilt feelings, and these feelings derived their satisfaction from the sickness. And the guilt feelings were obviously seated in the superego, which has monopolized all the individual's latent sadism:

> How is it that the superego manifests itself essentially as a sense of guilt (or rather, as criticism—for the sense of guilt is the perception in the ego answering to this criticism) and moreover develops such extraordinary harshness and severity toward the ego? If we turn to melancholia first, we find that the excessively strong superego which has obtained a hold upon consciousness rages against the ego with merciless violence, as if it had taken possession of the whole of the sadism available in the person concerned. Following our view of sadism, we should say that the destructive component had entrenched itself in the superego and turned against the ego. What is now holding sway in the superego, as it were, is a pure culture of the

death instinct, and in fact it often enough succeeds in driving the ego into death, if the latter does not fend off its tyrant in time by the change round into mania.[11]

VI

After 1920, the date of the appearance of *Beyond the Pleasure Principle,* psychoanalysis began to become an idealist philosophy. Hitherto it had rested on a scientific base and on clinical observations. Freud was suspicious of philosophical systems and until the twenties confined himself to the field of facts. He had introduced the principle of causality into mental life by demonstrating that apparently meaningless acts such as dreams or slips are determined by rigorous laws. The concepts he had formulated, such as the libido, repression and the unconscious, etc., were not arbitrary constructions, but in a most economical fashion bore witness to a whole series of normal or sick psychological phenomena. One attempted to interpret these phenomena by formulating the least possible number of abstract concepts.

The introduction of the theory of the death instinct to explain sadism, melancholy, masochism, aggression, and so forth, violates this principle of correct scientific strategy.

In *Beyond the Pleasure Principle,* Freud had attributed the cause for certain therapeutic failures to the compulsion to repeat. Three years later he enlarged this hypothesis and confirmed that patients did not want to be cured because their superego was opposed to it. Since the superego was the de-

---

[11]*The Ego and the Id,* Standard Edition of the Complete Psychological Works, vol. 19, p. 53.

pository for the death instinct, the analyst could only yield to it. The success that this theory met with from many psychoanalysts says a lot about the state of therapy at the time.

Sadism and masochism, which had always been a source of confusion to psychoanalysts, were explained in terms of the death instinct. Freud expounded his earliest theory on these two perversions in 1905, in *Three Essays on the Theory of Sexuality;* a second was discussed ten years later in *Instincts and Their Vicissitudes;* and a third was offered in 1924, in *The Economic Problem of Masochism.* He considered masochism to be the primary expression of the death instinct; while sadism represented the externalization of the death instinct. In both these perversions, the harmful effects of the death instinct are mitigated by its fusion with Eros. Masochism is distinguished as the "unconscious need for punishment" by the fact that in this latter case the death instinct is presented in its pure state, free of all erotic elements. The moral tortures that certain people inflict on themselves and that can lead them to suicide is explained henceforth by the cruelty which the superego can inflict on the ego. According to Freud, the death instinct can be neutralized in two different ways: when it is turned outward in the form of aggression toward others; or when it is combined with Eros.

The use of the death instinct theory to rationalize a reactionary concept of "human nature" proved to be scientifically sterile. Furthermore, after having been in fashion for a while, the very theory was increasingly disparaged. In a book which appeared in 1908, William McDougall maintained that instincts are the motors of behavior. As Holt says in *Animal Drive and the Learning Process:*

> Man is impelled to action, it is said, by instincts. If he goes with his fellows, it is the "herd instinct" which actuates him; if he walks alone, it is the "antisocial instinct"; if he fights, it is the instinct of "pugnacity"; if he defers to another, it is the instinct of "self-abasement"; if he twiddles his thumbs, it is the thumb-twiddling instinct; if he does not twiddle his thumbs, it is the thumb-not-twiddling instinct. Thus everything is explained with the facility of magic— word magic.[12]

To conclude this chapter on the contradictions and weaknesses of Freudian thought, let us consider the reservations that Karen Horney, an American psychoanalyst belonging to the so-called culturalist school of psychoanalysis, admits on the theory of the death instinct.

> Freud also fails to see that the assumption of a destruction instinct may appeal to people emotionally because it can relieve them of feelings of responsibility and guilt, and because it can free them from the necessity of facing the real reasons for their destructive impulses. . . .
> The disputable point in Freud's assumption is not the declaration that men can be hostile, destructive and cruel, nor the extent and frequency of these reactions, but it is the declaration that the destructiveness manifesting itself in actions and fantasies is instinctual in nature. The extent and frequency of destructiveness are not proof that it is instinctual.[13]

---

[12]Edwin B. Holt, *Animal Drive and the Learning Process* (New York: Henry Holt & Co., 1931), p. 4.

[13]*New Ways in Psychoanalysis* (New York: W. W. Norton, 1939), pp. 126–127.

And Horney concludes by saying:

> Equally harmful are the cultural implications of the theory. It must lead anthropologists to assume that whenever in a culture they find people friendly and peaceful, hostile reactions have been repressed. Such an assumption paralyzes any effort to search in the specific cultural conditions for reasons which make for destructiveness. It must also paralyze efforts to change anything in these conditions. If man is inherently destructive and consequently unhappy, why strive for a better future?[14]

VII

Reich hardly appreciated the change of atmosphere which followed the publication of *Beyond the Pleasure Principle*. The balance that psychoanalysis maintained between facts and theories was upset in favor of the latter. Analysts began to fabricate more and more literary constructions until psychoanalysis soon looked like an inverted pyramid. Reich describes this turn in the history of the psychoanalytic movement well:

> In 1923, Freud's *The Ego and the Id* was published. Its immediate effect on practice, which constantly had to deal with the patients' sexual difficulties, was confusing . . . In 1920 *Beyond the Pleasure Principle* had appeared, in which Freud, at first hypothetically, placed the death instinct on an even footing with the sexual instinct; more than that, he ascribed to it instinctual energy from an even deeper level. Those analysts who did not practise

---

[14]*Ibid.*, p. 132.

and those who were unable to comprehend the sexual theory, began to apply the new "ego theory." It was a sad state of affairs. Instead of sexuality, one now talked of "Eros." The super-ego, which was introduced as an auxiliary theoretical concept of psychic structure, was made use of by inept practitioners as if it were a clinical fact. The Id was "wicked"; the Super-ego sat there with a long beard and was "strict"; and the poor Ego tried to be a "go-between."[15]

Reich then shows how Freud's emphatic statement that "sexual repression is the principal cause of contemporary neuroses" became blurred in a philosophical fog:

Clinical discussions were fewer and fewer, and speculation took their place. Soon there appeared outsiders who had never done an analysis and gave high-sounding talks on the ego and superego, or on schizophrenias they had never seen. Sexuality became an empty shell, the concept of "libido" became devoid of any sexual content and turned into an empty phrase. Psychoanalytic communications lost their serious quality and showed more and more of a pathos reminiscent of the ethical philosophers . . . The atmosphere was "clearing." Slowly but surely it became cleared of the very achievements which characterized Freud's work. The adaptation to a world which shortly before had threatened the psychoanalysts and their science with annihilation, took place unobtrusively at first. They still spoke of sexuality, but no longer meant it.[16]

For his part, Reich rejected the death instinct

---

[15]*The Function of the Orgasm*, pp. 100–101.
[16]*Ibid.*, p. 101.

hypothesis. He asked Freud if one should take the hypothesis into account in clinical work. Freud re-assured him by replying that he could ignore it; advice which Reich and his technical seminar colleagues followed. He then began to fence clumsily with the theory's partisans:

> One had no use for such explanations if pains-takingly exact clinical presentations were made. Occasionally, one or the other death instinct theorist would try to make his opinion felt. I carefully abstained from any direct attack on this erroneous doctrine; clinical work itself would make it no longer viable.[17]

---

[17]*Ibid.*, p. 105.

Chapter VI

Entry into the Communist Party

A photograph of Reich taken in 1927, when he was thirty, shows an enormous man with wide shoulders and the look of a peasant. The expression on his face, with its suspicious eyes, high forehead, and full lips, has something stubborn and uncouth about it.

At the beginning of that year, a number of incidents took place in the little Austrian town of Schattendorf. During a meeting held by the Socialist Party, some adversaries opened fire on the participants, killing two and injuring several others. On July 14, the murderers were acquitted by a judge of the old order.

The next day at ten o'clock in the morning, Reich learned that the workers in Vienna had gone on strike to protest this verdict, that the police had intervened during a demonstration, and that there had been several more deaths. Reich rushed into the street. Passing by the police station, he noticed a large troop of policemen to whom arms were being distributed. He finally arrived at a wide boulevard where the workers were filing by on their way to the Justice Department. Reich joined them.

To their delight they arrived at the Justice Department to find it in flames. Having broken through the police barrier, some young workers had set fire to the archives. A pitched battle, with the hardier demonstrators fighting the police, was taking place in the middle of an excited rabble. The crowd hurled insults at the police, as it fell back in disorder into the side streets. The groups were reforming here and there. Mounted policemen tried to disperse the demonstrators, while ambulances carried away the dead and injured. Only four policemen were injured. Rumor had it that police stations were burning in town. Reich fled to a park and saw several people mowed down by machine guns. He ran home to fetch his wife, and they left immediately to return to the Justice Department.

Near the town hall they saw a cordon of armed policemen moving toward the crowd which was watching them without suspicion. When they were no more than thirty yards away, their officer gave the order to open fire. The crowd scattered in all directions, but dozens of bodies lay stretched out on the ground. Reich and his wife observed the massacre from behind a tree, and then returned home.

During the evening, calm returned to the center of Vienna, but incidents continued in the outskirts of town and lasted until the next day.

Wilhelm Reich was profoundly shaken by these events. In a long and lively chapter in his book *People in Trouble,* he tells of the scenes he witnessed during that day and the shock it had been to him. The behavior of the police, those "robots without souls," as he called them, had appalled him. That very day he joined the Communist Party.

In 1927, Reich was already a well-known psychiatrist. He had an important practice and earned a very good living. Despite the harassment that he and certain of his colleagues suffered, all the world recognized his intellectual qualities and the value of the work that he accomplished during his technical seminar.

As director of the technical seminar as well as Freud's assistant at the psychoanalytic polyclinic, he represented a good recruit for the little Austrian Communist Party. As soon as he had enrolled in the Party, he was invited to give lectures before audiences of progressive students and workers. At first he tried to explain to his listeners the fundamental principles of psychoanalysis. He realized very swiftly that this accomplished little because his listeners did not relate them to their everyday life.

One day he gave an account of the sexual condition of the masses and met with great success— the subject had struck a responsive chord in his audience. It should not be forgotten that Reich had been working in Freud's polyclinic for several years and knew a great deal about the difficulties facing neurotics, particularly those belonging to the Viennese proletariat. Within a few months, as he watched the sexual misery of the masses unfold before him, Reich was able to judge the extent to which concrete issues, such as infant education, conjugal relations, and sexual problems in general, awakened interest. He found that the young people had difficulty in finding sexual partners; either they did not have a room of their own and had to get by with making love on the sly or they masturbated. There was no contraceptive information available, and the population was ill-informed on the subject, with the inevitable result that young girls were inhibited by the fear of pregnancy. Illegal abortions, practiced in unbelievably unhygienic circumstances, were a social disgrace. Many couples were ill-matched, but the material difficulties of obtaining a separation forced them to continue living together, while their children bore the brunt of their accumulated rancor. In many working-class homes a new birth represented a catastrophe because of the costs that it involved. Reich wondered how many times the child was hated before it had even been brought into the world.

As far as sexual hygiene was concerned, the living conditions of the masses were as deplorable as the sanitary conditions had been during the Middle Ages. In Europe, epidemics of the plague or typhus had disappeared as sanitation improved and medical discoveries progressed, but neuroses had replaced them.

As he measured the extent of the collective sexual discomfort, Reich became skeptical about the efficiency of individual treatment. What was the sense of wasting one's time and efforts treating one's patients on the psychoanalyst's couch if society continued to manufacture neuroses with the speed of an assembly line? Furthermore, psychoanalytic treatment takes years and is only accessible to a privileged minority. From all the evidence, the prevention of neuroses appeared to be the most logical solution to the problem.

In 1927 Reich had the idea of organizing mental health centers in the outlying districts of Vienna where free consultations would be given. By advising parents on the education of their children, by enlightening adolescents on sexual physiology, and by recommending the use of contraceptives, Reich hoped to lower the number of neuroses. He mentioned it to Freud, who thought it was a good idea. But when Reich, who was already aware of the central role the family plays in producing neuroses, told him of his intention to attack this problem, Freud replied, "You're going to find you've opened up a hornet's nest."

In 1928 Reich, with the help of some doctors, put the first sexual hygiene centers on their feet in Vienna. They immediately flourished, confirming the crying need for advice and help in sexual matters. Here are a few examples of questions Reich was asked:

Why do the doctors refuse to help a pregnant woman who does not want or cannot have a child?

What must a husband and wife do if they want to make love but there are other people sleeping in the same room?

At what age can one begin to have sexual intercourse?

Is masturbation dangerous?

My daughter is four years old and she masturbates. I've punished her severely but it does no good. What can I do?

Do you allow your children to masturbate?

You talk of sexual health, but if your sixteen-year-old daughter brought her boyfriend home so that they could make love would you allow them to?

My husband does not satisfy me during intercourse because he comes too quickly. What should we do?

If sexual liberty were enforced, wouldn't it lead to chaos? I have the impression that my husband would leave me.

I'm sixteen and my parents have ordered me to be home by eight o'clock. I think they're too strict with me. Should I obey them?

In *The Function of the Orgasm* Reich cites some fifty similar questions that demonstrate the diversity of the sexual problems and their relationship to the social conditions.

Given the role played by the repression of infantile sexuality in the formation of neuroses, Reich wondered why parents continued to stifle their children's sex life. Daily he dealt with patients whose troubles stemmed from the family atmosphere in which they lived. The accumulation of these observations convinced him that the family is a nest of neuroses which cripples parents and children indiscriminately. Bit by bit he began to study the available sociological literature on the family.

Exactly at this time the English anthropologist Bronislaw Malinowski, and the psychoanalyst Ernest Jones, entered into an argument on the subject of the family. Malinowski had studied the customs of the Trobriand Islanders in the northeast of New Guinea. The Trobrianders are a matriarchy: the line of descent is passed through the mother; the child belongs to his mother's tribe and inherits his wealth and social position from his maternal uncle. The father brings up his children in a spirit of friendship, having no authority over them. It is the mother's brother who plays the role socially recognized as the representative of authority.

The relationship between parents and children in the Trobriand Islands differs from the relationship between parents and children in Europe. Malinowski had established that the Oedipus complex, as Freud had described it, did not exist. But Jones maintained that the Oedipus complex is a universal fact and that the whole matriarchal system of the Trobriand Islanders was, in effect, an attempt to repress the complex. In brief, Jones was arguing that the Oedipus complex conditioned the whole of the social structure and institutions of the Trobriand Islanders.

This discussion between a psychoanalyst and an anthropologist showed clearly the lack of relativism and sociological understanding in Freud's disciples. For these latter, the patriarchic family, such as exists in European civilizations, constitutes the norm for man-woman relationships. Psychoanalysts considered the Oedipus complex as a permanent and immutable fact present in all cultures. But Malinowski maintained that this was not so, that the Oedipus complex was bound to a very precise family structure. Reich was extremely interested in this controversy because it touched on his own preoccupations. As he studied Engels' book. *The Origin of the Family, Private Property and the State,* his doubts about the validity of the Freudian theory of civilization grew stronger.

Reich was intensely busy during the last three years he spent in Vienna from 1927 to 1930. He read all the Marxist classics, numerous books on economics, sociology, ethnology, and assembled the material for his own later books (*Der Einbruch der Sexualmoral, Geschlechtsreife, Enthaltsamkeit, Ehemoral,* etc.). He continued to lead the technical seminar, and in 1928 he became the assistant chief of the psychoanalytic polyclinic. In addition to this, he had to tend to his private patients; spent many hours each week in the newly formed sexual hygiene centers, and gave a great deal of time to political activities. One day Freud asked him if he were planning to continue working on so many fronts at the same time. Reich evaded the question. Since he frequently had arguments with his colleagues on political subjects and criticized the cultural concepts of psychoanalysis, he had the impression that they were trying to remove him from the positions he held in the Psychoanalytic Association and that Freud was beginning to find him a burden. This is, in fact, plausible; Reich was becoming something of a nuisance with his political affiliations and his insistence on the role of sexual frustration in the formation of neuroses.

Freud's opinion on the Soviet Union is interesting. Although he had not been generally hostile to the Russian Revolution (he even expressed the hope that the new regime "promised a better future") he did, however, prove skeptical about the "Soviet experience." In his opinon, the Bolshevik endeavor must fail because it is contrary to human nature for men to live in a libertarian society.

> Bolshevism hopes in the course of a few generations so to alter human nature that people will live together almost without friction in the new order of society, and that they will undertake the duties of work without any compulsion. Meanwhile it shifts elsewhere the instinctual restrictions which are essential in society; it

diverts the aggressive tendencies which threaten all human communities to the outside and finds support in the hostility of the poor against the rich and of the hitherto powerless against the former rulers. But a transformation of human nature such as this is highly improbable.[1]

A few line further on, Freud sums up his thoughts and advances an interesting theory:

... a sweeping alteration of the social order has little prospect of success until new discoveries have increased our control over the forces of Nature and so made easier the satisfaction of our needs.[2]

In holding that the private ownership instinct and aggressive tendencies will jeopardize any attempt to found a Communist society, Freud is talking like the man in the street. (In this regard Reich will maintain that aggressive tendencies, repressed in the unconscious, are not instincts, but reactions to sexual and economic frustrations.) On the other hand, when Freud voices his doubts on the possibility of a Communist society as long as men are obliged to work hard and their needs cannot be satisfied, his opinion conforms to the Marxist doctrine. According to Engels, Communism (that is, a society without state, without private ownership, without a currency, and without families) can only exist in societies that produce next to nothing (this is primitive Communism); or in societies which, having attained a very high level of technology, are able to

---

[1]*Complete Introductory Lectures on Psychoanalysis,* p. 644.
[2]*Ibid.,* p. 645.

enjoy their abundance with a minimum of work. Since this last condition was a long way from being realized in Russia, Freud's skepticism was justified.

In his book *People in Trouble,* Reich recounts some of his experiences as a militant Communist. He took part in the routine work—distributing tracts in working-class districts and in front of unemployment bureaus, giving speeches at meetings, etc. During a strike in 1928, he took care of the strikers' children. A fairly comic anecdote is worth repeating. The end of the twenties in Austria and Germany was marked by the rise of Fascism. On October 7, 1928, a large Fascist demonstration was scheduled to take place at Wiener-Neustadt, an industrial center about twenty-five miles from Vienna. The Socialist Party, which had seen its electoral positions crumble, responded by organizing a counter-demonstration. The Communist Party, no more than three thousand strong, decided to stage a demonstration counter to both the Socialists and Fascists by sending to Wiener-Neustadt a group of demonstrators belonging to a nominal association of militant workers, numbering some two hundred and fifty members, and to which Reich belonged. This decision was fairly rash since it meant lining up two hundred and fifty Communists against an anticipated forty thousand Fascist and Social Democrat demonstrators.

One beautiful morning, Reich said goodbye to his wife and children and left with his bag full of bandages and mercurochrome. Persuaded that they represented the spearhead of the working classes and its avant-garde conscience, the two hundred and fifty Communists had received orders to rally in small groups in Wiener-Neustadt, arriving there at different times. They had to spend the night at an inn because the demonstration was not to be held until the following day. Reich's group was to meet at the southern station in Vienna. The main concourse of that station was full of plainclothesmen who had been told to keep their eye on the counter-demonstrators. Some fifty Communists strolled about apparently oblivious of one another; all purchased tickets to the last stop before Wiener-Neustadt so as not to give themselves away. That evening they re-grouped at the inn placed at their disposal by a sympathetic Socialist, and spent the night in the ball-room. Unable to sleep, Reich began a conversation with a young comrade who had been among the last to arrive from Vienna. He learnt that for two years this man had lived on unemployment and was still expected to contribute to the upkeep of his mother. From time to time he managed to find temporary work, which was illegal. They spoke for several hours, eating sandwiches and boosting each other's spirits in preparation for the following day.

At seven o'clock in the morning someone looked out the window and saw a cordon of armed police-men encircling the inn. In the wink of an eye every-one was on his feet. A police officer came into the room and said in a Viennese dialect, "Come on, men, get your things together. The train for Vienna is waiting for you." This announcement was badly received. The policeman replied that he was very sorry but he was under orders to accom-pany them all to the station. After much palaver, the Communists appointed Reich to be their spokes-man. He told the policeman that they wanted to talk things over before they decided what they were going to do. The Communists were divided into two camps—some wanted to stay, while others maintained that it was madness, since they were unarmed. Reich was furious, thinking of the ambush into which they had fallen (they learned subsequently that the innkeeper had denounced them), and would not take part in the vote. He felt like fighting, but they were so unevenly matched that a confrontation with the police would have led to a massacre. Finally they resolved to give in. Walking in fours and surrounded by the police, they wended their way to the station singing the *Internationale*. Sleepy, disgruntled faces appeared at the windows along their route.

At the station a reserved train was awaiting them, with two policemen with fixed bayonets in front of each carriage. Everyone got on board and the train left. It went along for a few minutes until someone pulled the alarm cord. This incident was repeated several times. As they limped along toward the terminus, they suddenly realized that if they went all the way to Vienna, the police would be waiting for them and would take their names. To avoid this trap, they got out at the next to last station, somewhat afraid that their armed guard might try to stop them or even open fire. They escaped without incident, however, and covered the last few miles on foot.

Reich was rapidly becoming a well-known figure in the Communist Party. He went to all the demonstrations organized by the Party, marching with the unemployed and the workers. He was struck by their docility and lack of aggression. Demonstrations were authorized by the municipality; the participants had to follow a fixed itinerary and disband at a given point. Each time they passed in front of the university the Fascist students provoked them by singing nationalist songs. Only once, says Reich, did a group of demonstrators respond by breaking rank and going to thrash a few students. Even on that day, the majority of the demonstrators remained indifferent.

In 1929 and 1930, Austria was hit by a depression which threw thousands of workers into the streets. In 1930 there were 400,000 unemployed out of a total population of six million. Reich says that in Vienna people were literally dying of hunger. He asked himself how these unemployed, living in the most acute poverty, could pass before the luxurious store windows in the center of Vienna without reaction? Why did they not loot everything? How could they live so close to the Viennese middle classes without attacking them?

Their attitude toward the police reflected the same respectful fear of the established order. The police, said Reich, were identified with the state, whose uniformed protectors they were. They exercised their arrogance and their brutality on anyone they wished to impress. In dealing with demonstrators who were, in their opinion, running away, they used their nightsticks with abandon, and the fear that these inspired established the police in their role. But their authority was dependent exclusively on the behavior of the people they confronted and would cease to exist the minute the crowd rebelled. Unfortunately the crowd proved indecisive, and their enthusiasm waned as soon as the police appeared on the scene. The problem of authority and the examples of servility he frequently witnessed, caused Reich to wonder why people support an unsympathetic system. As a result he conducted a systematic investigation of the irrational behavior of the masses, a subject on which he would later write many brilliant and enlightening pages. Occasionally he met groups of people who were ready to do anything, but this was rare. One evening, after a meeting with some socialist workers, a young mechanic came to talk to Reich. This was the time when the law authorizing the government to take exceptional measures in time of trouble was being debated in parliament. The mechanic explained to Reich that he had formed a terrorist group with some friends. They had machine guns at their disposal and were prepared to occupy the center of Vienna and hold it as long as possible. Unfortunately his plan had little chance of success; the majority of the workers were hostile or indifferent. After some discussion, they rejected the plan.

Reich was becoming more and more absorbed by his work in the mental health centers, where he spent a great deal of time and money. In January 1929, seconded by four psychoanalysts, three gynecologists, and a lawyer, he added to his work load by founding six sexual hygiene clinics reserved exclusively for workers and employees. In addition to the consultations, a monthly lecture took place in selected districts of Vienna.

Reich's goal was to find an efficient method of preventing neuroses which depended heavily upon the parents' attitude toward their children's sexuality. The conversations he had had with many young people taught him in a few months things he would never have discovered otherwise. The majority of young people lived in a state of revolt toward adults and were already delinquent. Many of them had run away from home because their parents would not allow them to lead a free sex life. Those who remained at home were reduced to making love illicitly, in parks or in doorways, without being able to get undressed. Since they had no means of contraception, the fear of pregnancy added to these deplorable conditions. Premature ejaculation, from which many of the young men suffered, was caused by the atmosphere in which they conducted their sex lives. It is very simple, Reich says, to blame premature ejaculation on urethral eroticism or on an Oedipus complex; but when one is forced to make love fully clothed, fearing that one will be caught at any moment, ejaculation will occur too early, before the excitation has achieved a sufficiently high level, and will result in a chronic sexual stasis. Reich had an opportunity to treat the many young people whose neuroses stemmed from the repression of their sexuality. He established that although they had been more or less unstable in approaching puberty, their neuroses only developed after several years of sexual conflict. When the way to a normal and healthy sex life is blocked, the adolescent will regress to infantile neuroses. All the troubles of puberty stem from actual neuroses which are widespread in young people because of the limitations society imposes on their sexual activities.

At first Reich had planned to fight the neuroses by prevention rather than treating them when they had already taken hold—this is how doctors go about controlling an epidemic—but the causes of the neuroses were bound up with the social structure. For example, when a couple shared a room with other people, not in the least unusual in Viennese working-class districts at the time, it was impossible for them to lead a normal sex life. Such a situation is a breeding ground for neuroses, yet it was difficult to find a remedy for it. Behind the problem lay the housing shortage, the workers' condition, and the exploitation of the proletariat. Then again, adolescents came to Reich telling him that they wanted to make love but did not know where to go. Reich realized this latter problem had more far-reaching implications: why did society check young people's sexuality? What purpose did general sexual repression serve?

Everything pointed to the fact that if he hoped to eradicate the causes of neuroses he would have to attack the established order. His experience as a clinician had taught him that the lack of genital satisfaction provoked neuroses. Yet society did everything to prevent people from leading a healthy sex life. At the judiciary level, a whole arsenal of laws stood in the way of sexual liberty; abortion was prohibited; the sale of contraceptives was rigorously controlled; minors found guilty of having sexual intercourse were sent to reform schools or put under the surveillance of probation officers. Then there was marriage itself protecting the *ad hoc* legislation, the only form in which the society tolerated the realization of sexual needs. It seemed as though the laws governing divorce were drawn up expressly to complicate the lives of those who sought it, and this evidently helped to guarantee the stability of the family.

Existing legislation often placed Reich in an embarrassing position, especially when young people of fourteen or fifteen came to him asking for contraceptives, or when pregnant women wished to terminate their pregnancies.

With the young people, Reich says he had three possibilities: to preach abstinence to them; to suggest that they masturbate; or to give them contraceptives. But if they were caught making love they ran the risk of being sent to reform schools, or, in the very least, of a parental thrashing. (This kind of problem illustrates the unresolvable situation in which progressive psychologists found themselves. Either they decided to do a superficial patching up, by adapting the individual to an unfortunate social environment, or else they ran the risk of pitting the individual against his environment, which would eventually create additional difficulties for him).

After considerable hesitation, Reich adopted the principle of supplying the young people with contraceptives and giving them all the necessary information about the sexual act, but he put them on their guard against the risks of getting caught. As for the women who wanted abortions, there was no way out of their situation because of the law forbidding abortion. These women should never become mothers in the first place, says Reich. If they were married, they hated their husbands and cheated on them whenever possible. If they were single, they slept with a different man every week without deriving any satisfaction from it. All exhibited nervous disorders. They worked like slaves in the Viennese factories or as maids. At the end of the day they also had to take care of their own homes. They were incapable of loving a child or understanding him or of bringing him up correctly. The lot which was awaiting their future child was easy to imagine. In these conditions, says Reich, it would have been inhuman, cowardly, and medically unethical not to interrupt their pregnancy.

Thus when Reich found himself face to face with the full range of sexual disorders among the proletariat, he realized that it was foolish to hope to eradicate the roots of the neuroses without attacking the institutions which had engendered and were perpetuating this sexual misery.

Several movements for sexual reform did exist, all of which were trying, without much success, to cure the collective sexual distress. But, as we shall see in the next chapter, these organizations had not gotten to the root of the problem and only succeeded in adding to the difficulties.

Chapter VII

The Family as a Source of Sexual Misery

In September of 1930 Reich left Vienna to establish himself in Berlin. The preceding year he had taken a trip to the USSR and had returned enthusiastic.

His relationship with many of the Viennese psychoanalysts had been deteriorating since 1927, which explains, in part, his departure. Moreover, the workers' movement in Germany offered him a wider field of action.

During a meeting which took place at Freud's in December 1929, Reich made a statement on the prevention of neuroses. The other psychoanalysts present felt that Reich was trying to challenge them and provoke Freud. Reich had in fact raised a pertinent issue by asking if they intended to adhere to the fundamental theory of the sexual etiology of neuroses or if they were thinking of retracting. If they held to this theory, he continued, they must be ready to accept all the consequences; that is to say, they should recognize the part played by conventional morality and the antisexual legislation in the formation of nervous disorders. Referring to statistics obtained through the sexual hygiene centers, he exposed the frequency of neuroses in the Viennese population and said that to ignore them would be to behave like an ostrich burying its head in the sand. In conclusion he stated that psychoanalysis could not remain neutral before these problems. It had to come out on one side or the other.

Reich thus put the directors of the Psychoanalytic Association on the spot. But the direction in which psychoanalysis was moving was irreversible. From this day the rupture between Reich and the psychoanalytic movement was only a matter of time. It actually took place four years later.

In 1930, Reich published a book called *Sexual Maturity, Abstinence, and Marital Morality,* a revolutionary analysis of the family. This book was the beginning of a whole series of works on sociology and social psychology Reich was to write between 1930 and 1934. It went into several editions, the last of which, *The Sexual Revolution,* has been published in America.

In 1934, the French Communist Party published a translation under the title *La Crise Sexuelle* (*The Sexual Crisis*), although curiously enough Reich had been excluded from the German Communist Party the previous year. Doubtless this lack of coordination between the different branches of the Party can be explained by the local difficulties the German Communist Party was experiencing at the time.

In the last chapter we saw how Reich had first hoped to eliminate the social causes of neuroses by changing the public approach to sexuality and had then understood that there was no hope of sexual reform in a capitalist world.

In his book, *Sexual Maturity, Abstinence, and Marital Morality,* Reich demonstrates how out-of-date morality and sexual legislation were. A majority of the population led a sexual life which in one way or another fell foul of the social norms. This vacillation between the accepted values and reality triggered a sexual crisis which was insoluble as long as the existing social order was maintained.

Sexual reform has never been discussed to the extent it is today, Reich said. But in sexuality, as in politics, the reform obscures the true problems and deflects attention to secondary objectives. The goals of the sexual reformers do not get down to the root of the trouble. Their faintheartedness is reflected in how far they are behind the real state of affairs. For example, more and more young people, between the ages of fourteen and eighteen, have had sexual intercourse. Yet the movements are discussing the opportunity for sexual intercourse "between fiancés." Or again, despite the frequency of illegal abortions and the spread of contraceptive devices, the sexual reformers are timidly approaching the question of whether social criteria should be taken into account in authorizing abortion. If attempts at sexual reform lag behind life in this way, it is proof that they are based on an internal contradiction. Well-intentioned people hoping to introduce sexual reforms have not measured the abyss which separates the moral code and the laws from sexual reality; if they are aware of it, they are only proposing half measures.

Such sexual reforms run aground regularly because their aim is to consolidate marriage and the family while these institutions are the very origin of sexual misery. Since partisans of sexual reform are rarely revolutionaries, Reich continues, they hesitate to start a universal debate by questioning the value of marriage and the family and confine themselves to partial demands. The sexual problem is indissolubly bound to the authoritarian social structure and can only be changed by the destruction of the established order.

According to official morality, the sexual function may only be exercised in marriage. Society has thus grafted onto sexuality matters which are foreign to it, such as the question of inheritance and other economic interests, and which help to distort it.

What is more, marriage implies, at least theoretically, conjugal fidelity and ensures the chastity of single people, and this leads to exactly the opposite of what society finds desirable. Monogamy gives rise to adultery and the imposed chastity of young girls inevitably results in prostitution. Also, the difficulty of breaking conjugal ties is in contradiction to the needs of natural sexuality; the human being must have change and cannot be satisfied indefinitely with the same partner, which calls for the periodic renewal of sexual experiences. As Reich says, no one would dream of wearing the same clothes all year, or eating the same dish; yet morality does not consider it absurd to require that we know only one sexual partner during the whole of our existence. Finally, the prohibition of abortion protects marriage because if abortion were to become legal for both married and unmarried women, one would have to recognize the existence of extramarital relationships. Similarly, the moral obligation to marry a young pregnant girl would disappear and the marriage institution would be compromised. But legislation prohibiting the termination of pregnancies is cancelled out by the inevitable proliferation of illegal abortions, just as the prohibition of alcohol leads to bootlegging. In short, prostitution, adultery, and illegal abortions can be traced directly to the institution of marriage, and it can thus be argued that marriage is at the heart of sexual misery.

In the final analysis the problem of puberty—that is to say adolescent troubles, conflicts with parents, etc.—is also dependent on marriage. "In no other domain," says Reich, "has conservative ideology been able to influence sexology to the degree that it has affected the sexuality of adolescents." The manner in which psychologists and educators treat the question of youthful sexuality is like a conjuring trick; those in authority recognize that by definition puberty means a sexual coming of age, but they perform all sorts of contortions to show the young people that they have no need of love-making and that they must respect abstinence. All the sexual misery of the young stems from the chastity that society imposes upon them.

In our society, says Reich, adolescence is a period of psychological troubles, of family conflicts and scholastic problems. Parents ignore, or appear to ignore, with a mixture of hypocrisy and good faith, the reason for the strange sickness which strikes their children between the ages of thirteen and eighteen. By listening to the educators chatter or the parents lament, one could honestly believe that puberty is a type of disease like chicken pox or mumps.

Sociologists explain that young people's rebelliousness stems from the fact that society does not offer them enough responsibility. Doctors complete the erroneous picture by saying that the genital glands are secreting hormones which disturb the behavior of the young. (Puberty is then a biological problem!)

All this nonsense is merely playing the fish. Those who have kept a minimum of common sense know that the young are hemmed in by their intense sexual desires and the difficulty of satisfying them through sexual intercourse. All the troubles of puberty stem from this predicament. The fact is that from the age of thirteen, the young need to make love. The more conscious among them actually desire it. But the police, the church, and their parents are there to stop them. Adolescence today is a long and painful sexual agony. Apart from some resourceful young men, who succeed in sneaking through the barriers and finding a sexual partner, all other young people masturbate. But masturbation is only a substitute for the sexual act, and as soon as a sexual partner is found they renounce the practice of onanism.

Reich asserted that the reasons given to justify the prohibition of sexual relationships in young people do not bear scrutiny. Priests and pedagogues pretend that sexual intercourse is harmful to the young. In Europe in the 1930s the law authorized a girl of fourteen and a boy of sixteen to get married and have intercourse, but if they had not passed before a representative of the state before making love, they were sent to a reform school or a psychiatrist. It has also been said that abstinence will improve the young person's scholastic performance. Reich comments:

> It is argued that sexual intercourse of youth would decrease their achievements. The fact is—and all modern sexologists agree in this— that all adolescents masturbate. That alone disposes of this argument. For, can we assume that sexual intercourse would interfere with social achievement while masturbation does not?[1]

All things being equal, masturbation gives less pleasure than the sexual act and is burdened with guilt feelings that poison the life of the adolescent. The argument that the repression of juvenile sexuality will increase their work capacity is thus absurd because nearly all adolescents masturbate, undermining their psychological balance and ruining their capacity for concentration.

But then why are young people forbidden to make love? Reich argued that there must be a reason since society attaches so much importance to this prohibition.

To find the answer he says we need only speculate what the consequences would be if young people were permitted to indulge in sexual intercourse. Sexual liberty would spell an end to marriage. The shackles that prevent young people from realizing their sexuality lead them to look upon marriage as desirable. It is for this reason that the problem of puberty is bound to the institution of marriage.

A Russian doctor, Barash, has published statistics showing that a correlation exists between the

---

[1] *The Sexual Revolution* (Orgone Institute Press, 1945), p. 85.

frequency of adultery and the age at which the subject began to have sexual intercourse; the earlier he started the more likely is the possibility that he will cheat on his marriage partner. The repression of juvenile sexuality serves as a preparation for marriage, since its stability depends on the continence of the young:

> If, further, there is statistical evidence for the fact that *early sexual intercourse makes people incapable of marriage* (in the sense of conservative marriage morality, "one partner for life"), then the purpose of the demand for sexual abstinence is clear. It serves the purpose of *creating a sexual structure which makes people incapable of any sex life except that of a strictly monogamous compulsive marriage* and it makes them submit weakly to the demands of society.[2]

Reich now comes to the problems that face the married couple themselves. Normally their feelings would begin to cool off after a variable passage of time. If the partners are well matched, if they are orgastically potent, this period can last for several years. But, with some exceptions, the satisfaction that the couple derive from their relationship begins to diminish at a certain point.

Then there are two alternatives: either one of the partners feels the need to leave (eventually they both do); or he refuses to face the problem and represses the desire. If separation brings up complicated problems; if the couple have been steeped in bourgeois morality; or if they are afraid to be alone; there is little chance that they will allow

[2]*Ibid.*, p. 102.

themselves to become aware of the deterioration of their relationship. When they persist in living together in spite of the change in their feelings, they are following a course which is as well regulated as the movement of a clock, during which their life turns into a miniature hell. Their sexual relationship brings them less and less pleasure and becomes a duty or a dreary routine. The irritation that they feel toward each other is either overt or repressed, depending on their temperament. In any case, their hatred grows with each passing day. If it is unconscious, it is camouflaged by a reactive glaze of affection.

> This reactive affection born of hatred and attendant guilt feelings is the specific basis of a sticky attachment, and the very reason why people so often, even if they are not married, cannot separate, even if they have no longer anything to say to each other, and the continuation of the relationship is nothing but a mutual torture.[3]

This state of affairs, which is common in the majority of households, is due to the obstacles which stand in the way of sexual freedom. If sexual relations were perfectly fluid, that is to say if they could be formed and dropped according to the individual's taste, without economic, moral, or material obligations interfering, they would reflect only the feelings of the partners and nothing else. The institution of marriage is an efficient barrier against the founding of free sexual commerce, because it limits the autonomy of the couple and eventually compels

---

[3]*Ibid.*, p. 124.

them to live together, even if they are at swords' point or if they secretly detest each other. Coercive marriage, Reich pointed out, is an evil caricature of authentic monogamy founded on love.

In this way society interferes with the individual and makes it impossible for him to love properly. Nine times out of ten, what we take to be love consists of an infantile dependency, of the desire for security, or of the need for domination, submission, possession, etc. Jealousy, that stifling accompaniment of love, betrays a proprietary attitude toward the erring partner, reducing him to the rank of an object to which one considers one has sole rights; in other words, a jealous man or woman behaves like a proprietor fearing he will be dispossessed of his goods.

In addition, sexual repression appears to divide sexuality into two parts, of which one, tenderness, is socially acceptable; and the other, sensuality, is condemned. Hence comes this disassociation between affection and sexual pleasure which we often observe in male adolescents, and which leads them to live a double sex life; they nourish a non-physical (platonic) passion for a young girl whom they idealize, while they transfer their sexual desires to another young girl whom they consciously or unconsciously despise. This behavior is typical of the orgastically impotent, who make love without identifying the actual partner with the ideal partner; the sex object they hold in their arms and the ideal picture are not superimposed. Fantasies and a feeling of disgust or sadness disturb the sexual act.

It is important to note that Reich never preached the abolition of marriage and the family within the framework of our capitalist society. He never recommended that free love and sexual liberty could go hand in hand with capitalism. That would be as absurd as demanding the dissolution of the state, of the police, or of the currency, while maintaining capitalism. If the causes of neuroses are to be rooted out, capitalism must first be destroyed.

After having shown that sexual misery (neuroses, perversions, illegal abortions, youthful disturbances, etc.) stem from the family institution, Reich asked himself why society attaches so much importance to the family, and what are the functions that it fulfilled. Thus he went on to a critical analysis of the family starting with the writings of Engels, Freud, Morgan, Bachofen, and Malinowski.

Chapter VIII

The Family as Educational Apparatus

Reich read *The Origin of the Family, Private Property, and the State* carefully. In it Engels enumerates three functions which the family fulfills in a capitalist society:

1. The passing on of inheritances, which allows the bourgeoisie to perpetuate itself as a class. The riches that it accumulates augment from generation to generation and remain in its control.

2. The family may occasionally make up an economic production unit. This is still the case in the country where parents and children work on the family farm, and with small tradesmen.

3. The family represents the way the human species reproduces itself.

Engels demonstrates that as capitalism flounders, the family will dissolve as a matter of course; as a production unit it is already threatened by the growth of industry. In a Communist society, public services will replace household duties and take charge of the children's education. Finally, when private ownership disappears, the family will have lost its last reason for existing, since it essentially serves to pass on, through inheritance, the riches which belong to the parents.

Engels contended that monogamy as it exists today is no more than an evil caricature of the union based on love, and that it debases men and women alike. What is more, the present-day social inferiority of the woman helps falsify the relationship of the couple. Couples who come together in the society of the future will in no way be like those of today.

The disappearance of the family in Communist society, prophesied by Marx and Engels in the *Communist Manifesto* one hundred and twenty-three years ago, enraged the bourgeoisie. This topic still makes the reactionaries bristle.

In demonstrating that the unity of the family cell is acquired at the cost of repressions which give rise to neuroses, psychoanalysis similarly contains the germs of a criticism of the family institution. The painful Freudian truth is perpetuated from generation to generation at the heart of the family triangle—mother, father, children. On the other hand, while Engels stressed the passing on of inheritance, Freud placed the blame on the passing on of moral values. We have already seen that the Freudian model of the personality is made up of three factors: the ego, the superego, and the id. The superego is like an internal policeman, born of the constraints imposed upon the child by the parents and educators. Now, as Freud observed, educators bring up children according to the dictates of their own superegos. In these circumstances, he says:

A child's superego is in fact constructed on the model not of its parents but of its parents' superego; the contents which fill it are the same and it becomes the vehicle of tradition and of all the time-resisting judgments of value which have propagated themselves in this manner from generation to generation.[1]

And Freud continues several lines further on:

It seems likely that what are known as materialistic views of history err in underestimating this factor. They brush it aside with the remark that the human "ideologies" are nothing other than the product and superstructure of their contemporary economic conditions. That is true, but very probably not the whole truth. Mankind never lives entirely in the present. The past—the tradition of the race and of its people—lives on in the ideologies of the superego, and yields only slowly to the influences of the present and to new changes; and so long as it operates through the superego it plays a powerful part in human life, independently of economic conditions.[2]

Reich developed the idea contained in these lines to explain why the masses take so long to become aware of the economic realities and to explain their considerable inertia as seen in the habit of submission among the repressed. By combining the Marxist and psychoanalytic viewpoints on the family, he arrived at a libertarian synthesis which was rejected by both the Freudians and the Communists.

---

[1]*New Introductory Lectures on Psychoanalysis*, p. 531.
[2]*Ibid.*

The stability of all societies that are divided into social classes depends on the freely given consent of the exploited members of the community. If these latter spent their time questioning the established order and attempting to overcome the ruling classes by force, no social hierarchy would be viable. Thus the classes situated at the bottom of the social ladder must accept their condition, eventually losing all sense of being exploited. When this psychological transformation has been achieved, the dominance of the ruling classes is a *fait accompli;* it becomes an institution and is no longer regarded by the oppressed as an imposition. It is the classic process at the end of which the violence of the stronger is accepted by those on whom it is exercised and is taken for granted to be their right. The oppressed then behave like robots, programmed in such a way that they do not rebel against the established order. In extreme cases, the robots will go so far as to justify their condition; they rationalize it, shunning all thought of freedom and rejecting any progressive ideas. The ruling classes have no need to apply force to maintain their respect, except on the occasion of the sudden uprisings which do occur sometimes. Jean-Jacques Rousseau said that slaves lose everything in their chains, even the desire to escape from them.

Let us consider a flock of sheep grazing in a meadow surrounded by an electric wire. When a sheep has touched the wire once or twice and received an electric shock, the sight of the wire has become a signal that triggers an avoidance reaction. This reaction is reinforced if the sheep comes into contact with the wire again. There is no further need of shepherds or of barbed wire; the sight of the wire is sufficient to keep the flock in its enclosure. A *conditioned reflex* has formed. Psychologists use the diagram below to represent a conditioned reflex.

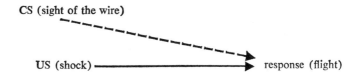

The unconditioned stimulus (US) has the power to trigger the response without previous experience. The conditioned stimulus (CS) acquires this power when it has been associated several times with the US and keeps the power even in the absence of the US. If the latter is introduced again, the response is strengthened. When a conditioned response begins to weaken (the extinction phenomenon) it is sufficient to reintroduce the CS to consolidate it (the reinforcement phenomenon). The conditioned reflex represents the most simple example of a phenomenon of experience which leads to the adoption of an elementary behavioral pattern.

Our social environment is made up of a net of invisible electric wires—the social norms, which we learn to respect through punishment and reward. In this way, the training of children within the family consists of instilling discipline into them, that is, the automatic submission to all figures of authority —parents, educators, policemen, employers, etc. By the end of his training, the individual has acquired not one conditioned response, as the sheep, but a totality of reactions which form a character structure adapted to the authoritarian system. The power of coercion with which the society invests its representatives of authority succeeds in reinforcing and serves to consolidate the attitudes of servility which have been arrived at during the course of the family training. In the final analysis, the goal of this education is to create robots who have interiorized the social constraints and who give in to them automatically:

> In a class society, the ruling class secures its position with the aid of education and the institution of the family, by making its ideologies the ruling ideologies of all members of the society. But it is not merely a matter of imposing ideologies, attitudes, and concepts on the members of society. Rather, it is a matter of a deep-reaching process in each new generation of the formation of a psychic structure which corresponds to the existing social order.[3]

A few lines further on, Reich sums up the role of the family:

> Because this order forms the psychic structure of all members of society, it *reproduces itself* in people . . . The first and most important place of reproduction of the social order is the patriarchal family which creates in children a character structure which makes them amenable to the later influences of an authoritarian order.[4]

Reich analyzed the role of the family and of antisexual morality in forming the character struc-

---

[3]*Character Analysis,* p. xxii.
[4]*Ibid.,* p. xxiii.

ture. In addition, he demonstrated that this character structure is reflected in irrational mass behavior; by which he means the proletariat's lack of class consciousness, its occasional adoption of reactionary doctrines, and the enthusiasm with which its people take part in imperialist wars.

It is unnecessary to emphasize the interest afforded by a Marxist psychiatrist's view of the tragic blindness of the masses which has already become evident on several occasions in the course of the last half-century.

We have seen that the family can form an economic production unit and serve to transmit inheritances. The development of capitalism has progressively eliminated the small tradesmen, who only exist today in marginal sectors like retail businesses, or small landowners who work their own land. The economic base of the family has thus narrowed, and in practice it is now confined to inheritance.

On the other hand, says Reich, the family's socio-political function has come into its own:

> Its cardinal function is that of serving as a *factory for authoritarian ideologies* and conservative structures. It forms the educational apparatus through which practically every individual of our society, from the moment of drawing his first breath, has to pass. It influences the child in the sense of a reactionary ideology not only as an authoritarian institution, but also on the strength of its own structure; it is the conveyor belt between the economic structure of conservative society and its ideological superstructure.[5]

---

[5]*The Sexual Revolution*, p. 72.

We have already remarked that the stability of social systems divided between the rulers and the ruled depends on the voluntary submission of the ruled and that this submission is obtained by the teaching of discipline. The family plays an important role in this training because it educates the individual at the moment he is most impressionable, that is to say, during his early years. The child learns first to obey his father, who is the representative of authority in the family; later this attitude of submission will be carried over to all bearers of authority. The concept of *generalization,* borrowed from experimental psychology, can help us understand this mechanism: when a dog has been conditioned to salivate on hearing a sound on a given frequency, he will also salivate on hearing sounds on neighboring frequencies. Similarly when an individual is dealing with a superior, it is as if he were face to face with his father and the traces which remain of his early training will facilitate his automatic submission. Seen in this way, the relationship between the father and his children is fundamental:

The basis of the middle class family is the relationship of the patriarchal father to his wife and children. He is, as it were, the exponent and representative of the authority of the state in the family. Because of the contradiction between his position in the production process (subordinate) and his family function (boss) he is a top-sergeant type; he kowtows to those above, absorbs the prevailing attitudes (hence his tendency to imitation), and dominates those below; he transmits the governmental and social concepts and reinforces them.[6]

---

[6]*Ibid.,* p. 73.

The connection between youthful rebellion against the family and rebellion against the established order is thus easy to trace:

It is not by accident that the attitude of adolescents toward the existing social order, pro or contra, corresponds to their attitude, pro or contra, toward the family. Similarly, it is not by accident that conservative and reactionary youths, as a rule, are very attached to their families, while revolutionary youths have a negative attitude toward their family and detach themselves from it.[7]

The family is then essential to the successful functioning of authoritarian systems because it passes on social attitudes that ensure the continuation of these systems. This, in turn, means the perpetuation of marriage, "society's permit to indulge in sexual intercourse."

Now, if sexual liberty were widespread, it would undermine the institution of marriage. Which is why authoritarian societies uphold a moral code condemning extramarital relationships.

If this moral code is to be upheld, each individual must have built-in sexual inhibitions. Parents begin this training by stifling their baby's sexuality, thus facilitating the repression of genital sexuality in adolescents because it is already associated with guilt feelings resulting from the repression of infantile masturbation (during the fifth year). Therefore the way to a healthy sex life for adolescents is barred by external and internal obstacles. The external obstacles are represented by the material difficulties the young people encounter when they want to make

[7]*Ibid.*, p. 72.

love—how to find a room or get hold of contraceptives, etc. It is unnecessary to dwell on the parents' role in this affair. As for the internal obstacles, they are made up of psychological blocks which can go so far as to suppress the perception of sexual needs. The internal and external obstacles are mutually reinforcing: the external factors strengthen the sexual repression, and the repression, in its turn, facilitates the action of these factors. The family is the motor which drives this circular process.

"In sum," says Reich, "the political function of the family, then, is twofold":

1) It reproduces itself by crippling people sexually. By perpetuating itself, the patriarchal family also perpetuates sexual repression with all its results: sexual disturbances, neuroses, psychoses, perversions, and sex crimes.

2) It creates the individual who is forever afraid of life and of authority and thus creates again and again the possibility that masses of people can be governed by a handful of individuals.[8]

Thus the family gains for the conservative individual its peculiar significance as a fortress of that social order in which he believes.

---

[8]*The Sexual Revolution,* p. 114.

Chapter IX

Irrational Mass Behavior

1. The False Consciousness

Marx and Engels formulated a principle of sociological definition which contemporary social scientists still use—the way of assessing a group of people is determined by their living conditions. For example, the political attitudes, moral values, and artistic tastes of a social class reflect its material situation.

A distinction can be drawn between the ruling classes and the oppressed by the way in which they conduct themselves in society. The ruling classes cannot picture the state of the world as it stands because this would require them to recognize that their supremacy is contingent upon the whole society. Their ideology has always been to justify the established order by assuming that it is a constant factor. The bourgeoisie, for example, has a fixed vision of the world which denies historical evolution, putting forward its own values as the accepted values of society. No ruling class can, in effect, allow itself to recognize that one day its reign must end.

On the other hand, one could expect that once the proletariat becomes aware of its condition it will fight to gain supremacy. A glance at the history of the workers' movement shows that this theory is not borne out by reality.

The theory that the working classes clearly understand their own interests, and act in consequence, is inherited from the old rationalist psychology of the eighteenth century. We see this psychology repeated by the liberals who believe that the citizens' political choices are dictated by rational motives. The liberals hold that when an individual arrives at the voting booth, he knows the programs of each party on the ballot and votes according to this knowledge.

These theories are belied by the facts. Today we know that neither the behavior of the electorate, nor the behavior of the consumer, nor the behavior of the oppressed classes is rational. Advertising men are well aware that for the most part unconscious factors determine the consumer's choice. That is to say that when one asks a housewife why she chose one brand of soap over another, the reasons she gives are not the true ones (even if she gives them in good faith).

The advertising agencies' success has led the bourgeois parties to profit from their services in organizing electoral campaigns.

If a linear relation did exist between the proletariat's consciousness and its economic exploitation it would mean, all other things being equal, that a rise in the cost of living would trigger pressure for a wage rise, and in turn, that the higher wages would be reflected by a lessening of the working classes' militancy. This plan is simplistic because it lays the blame for the living conditions of working classes squarely on economic oppression and assumes that the working classes are conscious of the oppression. Engels had already exploded this myth. Everything that spurs man into action must come from his brains, he said, but the form this impulse takes in the brain varies according to the circumstances.

Reich reasoned that there must be some factor barring the working classes' awareness of the fact that they are being exploited. He advanced the theory that the working class is steeped in the bourgeois cultural environment. Radio, newspapers, and television are all in the hands of the bourgeoisie and help spread its ideology to all levels of society. It is thus exposed to the daily contamination of the dominant ideology. But he knew that this does not explain why it submits on a long-term basis without throwing off the bourgeois yoke. If one believed that this is the only reason, one would fall into voluntarist ideology, which holds that intellect has the power to govern material situations by annulling the effect of the economic variables. A closer examination is necessary to see what factor in the proletariat's life style paralyzes its will to protest.

In the first chapter of his book *The Mass Psychology of Fascism,* Reich outlines the broad facts of the problem of class consciousness and shows that psychoanalysis can help to resolve it. He begins by stating that the Fascist success in highly industrialized countries has cast doubt on the validity of the fundamental concepts of Marxist sociology. In effect, once the economic situation in Europe was ripe for a revolution, the worker's movement broke down. Instead of revolution there was Fascism, that most virulent expression of reactionary politics, which corrupted Europe. The defeat of the worker movement was preceded by the failure of the Second International, by the downfall of the Spartakist Revolution, and the crushing of the Hungarian commune of Bela Kun. Reich blamed the vulgar Marxists who had drained Marxism of its scientific content. It is sufficient to compare one page of Marx or Engels with a book written by a Communist to see that Marxism had degenerated into a sterile theory, dependent upon economic determinism. (Economic determinism is a doctrine which reduces the concrete existence of man to its economic components, like buying power, the fluctuations of salaries, the rate of unemployment, etc.)

To these "Marxists," the Fascist victory was incomprehensible:

> This vulgar Marxism contended that an economic crisis of the magnitude of that between 1929 and 1933 must of necessity lead to the development of a Leftist ideology in the masses. Even after the defeat in January 1933, its representatives continued to talk of a "revolutionary upsurge." In reality, the economic crisis had —contrary to their expectations—led to an extreme development of a reactionary ideology in the masses.[1]

The discrepancy between the economic infrastructure of advanced capitalism and the impotence of the proletariat to fulfill its historic mission to overthrow capitalism must be explained. All the

---

[1]Wilhelm Reich, *The Mass Psychology of Fascism* (Orgone Institute Press, 1946), p. 5.

economic conditions were ripe for a Socialist take-over; the capital was concentrated in monopolies; the development of the world economy was hampered by customs regulations and national frontiers. In Reich's time capitalism had just suffered an enormous economic crisis which had pointed up the system's inability to resolve its internal contradictions. The economic machine was turning at fifty percent of its production capacity. Coffee was burned; the crops were destroyed; and thousands of pigs butchered to raise world prices; while in Europe and the U.S.A. millions were out of work, and the other workers were living in poverty. We were, says Reich, at the crossroads between socialism and barbarianism, and the working class chose barbarianism. From a rational point of view, one could have expected a revolutionary response from the impoverished masses. Instead of that they put Hitler in the saddle. Thus we come to the existing discrepancy between the condition of the working classes and their conservative ideology. When the masses are politically conscious of their condition, they act in a rational way which needs no psychological explanation. For example, when a starving man steals a loaf of bread, or when workers living in poverty decide to call a wildcat strike, their behavior is rational and self-explanatory. On the other hand, what social psychology must explain is not

. . . why the starving individual steals or why the exploited individual strikes, but why the majority of starving individuals do *not* steal and the majority of exploited individuals do *not* strike. Socio-economics, then, can satisfactorily explain a social phenomenon when human thinking and acting serve a rational purpose, when they serve the satisfaction of needs and directly express the economic situation. It fails, however, when human thinking and acting *contradict* the economic situation, when, in other words, they are *irrational*.[2]

Reich then tackles the problem of the reaction of ideology on its economic base. According to Marxist doctrine, ideological superstructures react upon the social infrastructure which gave birth to them. This shows that economic factors determine the social conditions in which people live; that these conditions are reflected by their brains in the form of ideas; and that men then act in accordance with these ideas to change their lives. Reich attacks the vulgar Marxists who underestimate the action in exchange for the ideology on its material base. The Communists, for example, repeat in parrot fashion that economic infrastructures and ideological superstructures interact, but they have never tried to explain precisely, with the help of scientific psychology, how a political doctrine spreads through a whole nation. The eruption of Nazism on the German political scene and its rapid spread to all social classes has shown that a reactionary ideology can set a large industrial country in motion. The retroaction of the ideology on the economic base can then prevail, at least temporarily, over the action of the economic factors. By ignoring the role of the "subjective factor" in history, the Communists believe themselves to be very materialist, but they are in fact falling into superficial ideology. Each time the working classes behave in a manner which belies their social oppression, the Communists say that the class

---

[2]*Ibid.*, p. 15.

has been deceived, that it lacks class consciousness, etc., or they deny the failure of the workers' movement by saying that all is going well, and that they are going from victory to victory. In brief, vulgar Marxists are incapable of explaining the contradiction between the economic frustrations endured by the proletariat and its lack of aggression.

Daniel Geurin, author of the best historical and economic study of Fascism, arrived at exactly the same conclusion:

> The degenerate Marxists, however, believe it is very "marxist" and "materialist" to disdain human factors and be interested only in the material and economic factors. They accumulate figures, statistics, and percentages; they study with great accuracy the profound causes of social phenomena. But by failing to study with the same care the way in which these causes *are reflected in the consciousness* of man, they miss the living reality of these phenomena.
>
> Hence, if they are interested only in the material factors, they understand absolutely nothing of the way in which the privations suffered by the masses are transmuted into a religious aspiration.[3]

To fill in this gap (that is to say, illustrate the role and the nature of the subjective factor in history), Reich created a social psychology, based on Marxism and psychoanalysis, which explains how an ideology takes shape in people's minds as a result of their social conditions, and how this ideology influences the masses. We have already seen that the

---

[3]*Fascism and Big Business* (New York: Pioneer Publishers, 1939), p. 69.

psychological explanation is superfluous when the behavior of the exploited masses is rational, that is, when they respond to their poverty by riots and uprisings. Thus, says Reich, "collective psychology must begin when the immediate socio-economic explanation proves abortive."

When he says that an ideology has a retroactive effect on its material base, Reich means that this ideology takes hold of men and makes them act in an unexpected fashion. And that once it becomes part of mass behavior, it is a material force. Reich asked himself how a reactionary doctrine could spread through a social class or through a whole society: the doctrine must fit in with a certain collective mentality, what Reich calls the "character structure of the masses." Let us take the example of the 1914–18 War. It involved a confrontation between French, English, and German Imperialism. Yet it was necessary that the masses be prepared to fight. They were. Those who fought on the front were fighting to conquer industrial zones and to ensure the European hegemony of their national bourgeoisie. But they did not know it. If one had asked a French worker why he had been mobilized, he would have replied that it was to defend France against the German barbarians or to save civilization. The problem is to understand how the proletariat could have been carried away by nationalist fervor and entered with enthusiasm into an affair that was no concern of theirs. Idealistic reasons are always put forward—the failure of the Second International, for instance. But, as Reich remarked, we should ask ourselves why the proletariat allowed itself to be betrayed.

Reich demonstrates that reactionary ideologies take hold of the proletariat easily because they fall on fertile character terrain. The collective character structure represents the subjective factor in history, and thus irrational mass behavior can be explained. We cannot take Marx and Engels to task for not having recognized it because the only way to understand it is through psychoanalysis, which did not exist in their time:

> The character structure of acting man, the so-called "subjective factor in history" in the sense of Marx, remained unexplored: Marx was a sociologist and not a psychologist, and there was, in his day, no scientific psychology. Thus the question remained unanswered as to why people, for thousands of years, have tolerated exploitation and moral degradation, in brief, slavery.[4]

The vulgar Marxists consider the workers as adults who hire out their labor to a capitalist and who are exploited. Reich agrees with this definition but says that one must take into account the social conditions of the worker if one wishes to understand his political attitudes. Among other things this means that he has had a childhood, that he has been educated by his parents, that he has a wife and children of his own, sexual needs, and family conflicts. Why should these factors be overlooked when the behavior of the working classes is in question?

2. Sexual Repression

The unity of the family cell depends upon the children being obedient to their parents. We have already seen that in learning to obey their parents,

---

[4] *The Mass Psychology of Fascism*, p. 20.

the children also learn obedience per se. The results obtained during the family training are carried over to all situations where the adult finds himself faced with an official superior. In punishing their children who masturbate and controlling the time their daughter returns home each evening, parents make sexual repression part of this family training. In order to adapt to the family environment, young people must then repress their sexuality. (Conversely, if their sexual needs are fulfilled, the young people appear to be in revolt against the parents. When a young girl returns home at six o'clock in the morning, she is defying her parents.)

Punishment teaches children to obey and forces them to give up sexual pleasure. Each time that the child is caught playing with his sexual organs, he is hit or threatened; when he is impertinent, he is reprimanded. In this way punishment succeeds in associating feelings of anxiety with the forbidden behavior. The anxiety which accompanies the expression of sexual needs comes from the same source as the anxiety which is aroused by rebellious impulses because sexuality and rebelliousness were indiscriminately repressed by the educators. To escape this anxiety, the child represses all those needs whose expression leads to punishment. In other words, the repression of sexuality is confused with the repression of all rebellious inclinations. In the end, the child is frightened by his sexual desires and by his tendency to revolt, and he stops the instincts from revealing themselves.

Reich then turned to an examination of the effects of these repressions. It is an established fact that repression is a psychological process which suppresses the perception of a need, an idea, etc. If the repression is total, the individual loses all consciousness of what he is repressing. But he has to use up a great deal of energy to arrive at this point. For repression is a costly process; the repressed impulses do not cease to exist; they lose none of their dynamism, and continue to lead an underground life in the unconscious. This means that the individual must constantly be defending himself against them by draining his psychological potential. Beyond the obvious neuroses and psychoses, this results in a narrowing of consciousness, a weakening of the mental faculties, and a lessening of the ability to concentrate. The consciousness atrophies and becomes a mere flicker.

Reich places all this in its sociological context:

> Suppression of the natural sexuality in the child, particularly of its genital sexuality, makes the child apprehensive, shy, obedient, afraid of authority, "good," and "adjusted" in the authoritarian sense; it paralyzes the rebellious forces because any rebellion is laden with anxiety; it produces, by inhibiting sexual curiosity and sexual thinking in the child, a general inhibition of thinking and of critical faculties. In brief, the goal of sexual suppression is that of producing an individual who is adjusted to the authoritarian order and who will submit to it in spite of misery and degradation.[5]

In this passage Reich establishes:

1. That sexual repression creates individuals who are terrorized by authority, and

2. That sexual repression, which results from the interiorization of sexual needs, weakens the

---

[5]*Ibid.*, pp. 24–25.

ego because the individual who must constantly invest energy in stopping the conscious expression of his sexual desires is not allowing himself to realize his full potential.

Reich tirelessly emphasized the social function of sexual repression. It trains the character to submit to authority and to fear liberty; resulting in the conditions which allow the enslavement of the masses to continue from generation to generation.

The child adapts, then, by trial and error to his family environment. When he masturbates he is punished, and he stops playing with his sexual organs. When he differs with his parents, he is chastised again and no longer dares stand up to them. And thus sexual repression is identified with the fear of authority. When the child appears gentle and obedient, he is rewarded. Little by little his personality builds itself through these exchanges. Character traits emerge, consolidate and will remain for the whole of his life. The first imprints that society leaves on the organism are indelible. The character represents, as it were, the history of the childhood which has been crystallized into the individual's behavior. In order to adapt to the family environment, the child represses his sexual needs and the hatred of his parents. Little boys achieve these repressions partly by identifying with the paternal image, foreshadowing the time when, as adults, they will identify with the authority of the state, of the firm where they work, etc. In effect, the father is the state's representative within his family. Identification with the paternal image and the attitude of servility which the son adopts toward his father heralds an ulterior identification with all forms of authority.

In order to neutralize his sexual needs and hatred of his parents, the child overcompensates for these attitudes. Therefore, by the time he has reached adulthood, the unconscious revolt against his father is masked by extreme submission to all forms of authority; and the fear of expressing his sexual needs has given rise to prudishness. Everyone is familiar with the frustrated old women and dried-up curates who passionately seek out the least sign of sexual excitement in children. They are so busy not thinking of sexual matters in themselves that they attack anything that evokes sexuality in others.

Thus we return to the character armor that Reich had discovered in his patients. It should be recalled that this armor is the totality of the defenses built up by the individual against his repressed needs. It is reflected in his behavior and helps diminish his psychological tensions by damming up in the unconscious anything that might arouse anxiety. Basically, the individual is a machine that functions in such a way as to keep anxiety at its lowest possible level.

> The result of this process is fear of freedom, and a conservative, reactionary mentality. Sexual repression aids political reaction not only through this process which makes the mass individual passive and unpolitical but also by creating in his structure an interest in actively supporting the authoritarian order.[6]

The character armor, already formed by the end of infancy, will only grow harder in the course of

---

[6]*Ibid.*, p. 26.

time. In order to endure his existence within the family, this state in miniature, the child has had to repress his sexuality and rebellious instincts against his parents. Since adult life similarly demands that the individual give way to authority and renounce sexual pleasure, it is, in a way, prolonging the infantile condition. To tolerate all the worries and privations of our everyday life, we must be protected against the world and against everything in ourselves which kicks against the life we know. Otherwise existence would be unbearable.

Some animals have adapted themselves to their surroundings by forming a hard shell that protects them at the same time as it imprisons them. The human being has used a similar method to adapt himself to his social environment.

The results of an inquiry conducted several years ago in the United States by T. W. Adorno on the authoritarian personality confirm Reich's conclusions. According to some sources, Adorno knew Reich in Germany during his Association for Sexual Politics period.

Adorno's team used five criteria to define what it called the "authoritarian personality":

1. The individual has a hierarchic view of human relations and exhibits great deference toward his superiors.
2. He depersonalizes human relations. He puts people "in their place" and expects similar treatment.
3. He is very conventional about correct behavior. Conformity is, in fact, one of his dominant character traits.
4. He exercises strict control over his impulses.

5. He is intolerant, morally rigid, and lacks the ability to adapt.

In studying the family histories of their subjects, Adorno's team of researchers discovered that they had the following points in common: their parents were strict, intolerant and showed a marked moral rigidity. They expected strict obedience from their children. They held themselves up to be ideal models (which can be interpreted partly as hostility toward the child and partly as a need for justification). The child submits to this system of injunctions and orders, represses his aggression toward authority, and becomes a servile little being who grovels before all bearers of authority. Later, he will project on to his subordinates the hate that is boiling up inside him; he is suspicious of others, repeats continually that people must be kept in hand, etc.

What Reich calls an authoritarian character structure tallies with the above description. He established that this character type is frequently found in the middle classes. Small tradesmen and employees often have a rigid moral code based on honor and duty to justify their colorless existence. They make a virtue of necessity. Depending on the political/cultural context, these people will either make good noncommissioned officers, become Fascists, or bureaucratic Communists.

The atmosphere in working-class families is generally less obsessive, and the parents tolerate their children's sexuality more easily. But it is only a difference in degree. The major obstacle preventing the development of revolutionary movements in the USSR, the U.S.A., and in Europe is the authoritarian family manufacturing slaves through the perpetuation of sexual repression. If there were no slaves there would be no slave drivers.

An individual's neurotic character structure will hinder his consciousness of class interests. The fear of freedom, the anxiety of being without a leader, the guilt provoked by enjoying oneself, ruin any attempts at social emancipation.

Now we understand a basic element of the reaction of ideology on the economic base. *Sexual inhibition alters the structure of the economically suppressed individual in such a manner that he thinks, feels, and acts against his own material interests.*[7]

When Reich was treating patients he realized that they were mobilizing all their defense mechanisms against him. They clung to their neurotic balance and were afraid when the psychiatrist touched upon the repressed impulses. Similarly, revolutionary proposals slide off the character armor of the masses because they recall all the impulses that the people have had to smother in order to endure their brutalization.

It would be a mistake to believe that the masses do not revolt because of a lack of information on the mechanics of economic exploitation. In reality, revolutionary propaganda, explaining the social injustices and irrationality of the economic system to the masses, falls on deaf ears. People who get up at five in the morning to go to work in a factory and who must also spend two hours a day in a subway or suburban train, can adapt to this existence only by refusing to consider anything that is likely to cast doubt on their way of life. If they realized they

---

[7]*Ibid.*, p. 26.

were wasting their lives in the service of an absurd system, they would commit suicide or they would go mad. To avoid facing this painful truth, they justify their existence and rationalize it. They repress everything which could upset them and develop a character structure adapted to the conditions in which they live. At this point, the idealist approach of explaining to people that they are oppressed serves no purpose because they have had to suppress the realization of this oppression in order to be able to live with it. Revolutionary propagandists often say that they want to enlighten the people; experience shows their efforts are rarely crowned with success because they are going against all the unconscious defense mechanisms and various rationalizations that the people have made so as not to become aware of their exploitation and of the emptiness of their lives.

3. The Historical Origin of Sexual Repression

When did antisexual morality first make its appearance in history? Reich wrote a large book *Der Einbruch der Sexualmoral* in answer to this question. Today this book is unavailable in any language. It was never translated into English.

Reich referred to Engels, Morgan, Bachofen, and Malinowski in establishing the social and economic conditions which gave rise to sexual repression.

He adapted two of Engels' fundamental theses on the social life of primitive peoples: first, the existence of a mode of production based on the collective ownership of the working tools (which Engels calls "primitive Communism"); and second, the preponderance of women over men, which is seen in matriarchal societies. Let us examine briefly how primitive Communism and mother right came about. Engels maintained that meager profits which did not allow the establishment of a permanent surplus of riches that could be appropriated by a nonproductive class gave rise to primitive Communism. Since the tribe produced just enough to subsist on, no overproduction existed that a fraction of the community could have turned to its own advantage. When barbarianism came to an end and man began to find uses for iron, to domesticate and breed animals, and to cultivate the land, the work returns increased considerably. From the moment that "two arms produced more than one mouth could consume," the creation of a social overproduction became possible. This permanent surplus of food and material goods upset the balance of primitive Communism, giving way to a system of production based on the exploitation of slaves.

The sexual life in primitive Communist societies was characterized by a very great freedom and by the superior position women held in the tribe. Given this free sexual commerce, the facility with which couples formed and broke up, there was no way of determining the paternity of a child. On the other hand, the mother was always known; the line of descent could therefore be passed only through the maternal side. Bachofen coined the phrase "mother right" to designate the matrilineal system.

According to the division of labor, the men were expected to furnish food and the necessary tools while the women took care of the household. The development of husbandry and slavery put a new source of wealth into the men's hands, bringing them additional importance within the matriarchal society. Little by little the women's place was reduced and the men benefited from this reversal of power. According to Engels, the men wanted their own children to profit from their increased wealth, and therefore matrilineal descent was invalidated. The end of mother right, which Engels calls "the great historical defeat of the female sex," was, then, the result of technical progress which, because of the division of labor, brought additional economic power to the men, and this was found to be incompatible with the social supremacy of women. The contradiction between production methods based on the use of slaves and agriculture on the one hand, and a matrilineal society on the other, shattered this latter which was replaced by the patriarchal family where women were dominated by men. In summary, primitive Communism was dissolved for economic reasons, destroying mother right and establishing masculine sovereignty.

The advent of masculine domination (the patriarchy) radically transformed society. A class of polygamous chiefs was formed; their wives were kept cloistered to be used as instruments of pleasure and reproduction. From now on women were confined to secondary roles; their debasement and their subjugation to men began at this time. Reich has shown that antisexual morality rose with patriarchy. His argument may be summarized as follows: The leaders of primitive communities were in possession of the political power, and a large part of the society's wealth was concentrated in their hands. Since these leaders bequeathed to their children the riches they had accumulated, they had to be sure their wives were faithful. Patrilineal filiation requires the chastity of women. Thus sexual life within ruling class families was strictly regulated.

Reich was surprised to discover a fine example of the effects of material interests on sexual life among the Trobriand Islanders. The example corroborated his theory that sexual repression first appeared in ruling-class families when they were in the process of formation. The Trobriand Islanders have two forms of marriage: If a girl marries her first cousin, her mother's brother's child, it is considered to be a good match. All other marriages are more or less disparaged.

This custom appears bizarre and contrasts deeply with the very great sexual freedom that the Trobriand Islanders enjoy. (They still have a matriarchal system.)

Thanks to the custom of paying dowries, the chiefs add to their wealth by accumulating those paid by their wives' brothers, and recovering others they themselves paid to their sisters if their sons make a good marriage—that is, if they marry their cousins. A good marriage thus succeeds in bringing back to the family the riches that went out of it in the form of dowries.

Children destined for good marriages are subjected to unaccustomed sexual restrictions. They are not allowed to indulge in sexual games like all the other little Trobrianders, and their sexual education resembles that taught in Western societies—Europe, USSR, U.S.A. As a result of this obsessive morality, which prepares them for good marriages resulting in the accumulation of dowries by the polygamous leader's family, they fall prey to neuroses. There is, then, an apparent correlation between the economic power of the ruling class and the sex life of its members. They may no longer marry whom they wish, for fear of squandering their heritage. Only profitable unions, from the material point of view, are permitted. In other words, economic interests—the growth of riches within the ruling class—become confused with sexuality and cause sexual freedom within the class to be restricted.

In addition, the patriarchal system demands that women be faithful to their husbands because this is the only guarantee the men have that their children are really theirs. This is to say that a moral code condemning extramarital relations for women necessarily accompanies a patriarchy. (Even today, society tolerates a husband's infidelity far more readily than a wife's, and turns a complacent eye on the male Don Juan, while it severely condemns female adultery).

In brief, according to Reich, sexual repression arose with private ownership and the setting up of a patriarchal system. It, therefore, has a well-defined historical origin and did not simply fall out of the heavens. Reich had already arrived at these conclusions when he heard of Malinowski's studies on the sex life of the Trobrianders.

Since Malinowski's work confirmed what Reich had already discovered, he was delighted by it.

The first thing that strikes the European observer is the great sexual liberty enjoyed in the Trobriand Islands:

> Every man and woman in the Trobriands settles down eventually to matrimony, after a period of sexual play in childhood, followed by general license in adolescence, and later by a time when the lovers live together in a more permanent

intrigue, sharing with two or three other couples a communal "bachelor's house."[8]

Malinowski was equally struck by the almost total absence of psychological troubles. He says he never once encountered a nervous tic, a neurosis, or a sexual perversion. Homosexuality in particular was almost nonexistent.* He was familiar with psychoanalysis and understood the relationship between their sexual liberty and the rarity of neuroses:

> Another point which might be interpreted in favor of the Freudian solution to this problem is the correlation of sexual perversions with sexual repression. Freud has shown that there is a deep connection between the course of infantile sexuality and the occurrence of perversion in later life. On the basis of his theory, an entirely lax community like that of the Trobrianders, who do not interfere with the free development of infantile sexuality, should show

---

[8]Bronislaw Malinowski, *Sex and Repression in Savage Society* (London: Routledge & Keegan Paul, Ltd.), p. 9.

*According to psychoanalytic terminology, homosexuality is a perversion. But this term does not imply any value judgment. Not only have their been many homosexual geniuses (Leonardo da Vinci, Shakespeare, André Gide, Eisenstein, etc.) but as Reich says:

"As long as sexual education creates homosexuals, no one should be concerned if these men live in this way without harming anyone, and if they conduct themselves properly in society.

"The assertion that homosexuality is deviant and does not stem from natural causes gives no one the right to condemn or punish those involved. We must try to cure the homosexuals who wish to escape from their peculiarity because they are suffering or because it does not give them sufficient pleasure, but under no circumstances should anyone be forced out of it." (*The Sexual Struggle of Youth.*)

a minimum of perversions. This is fully confirmed in the Trobriands.[9]

Since then, missionaries have wrought havoc with this state of affairs. They have separated the boys from the girls, confining them in boarding schools, and are teaching them the Christian religion, giving them a little general instruction, and, naturally, imposing Western principles and discipline upon them. As Reich said, missionaries are the forerunners of the colonial system.

The contrast between matriarchal societies where there is no central authority and where sexual liberty goes hand in hand with well-balanced, healthy, and spontaneously friendly human beings, on the one hand, and patriarchal societies which produce nervous wrecks as a result of sexual repression, on the other, is striking.

The reinstatement of antisexual morality in the USSR illustrates the tie which exists between dictatorships and the authoritarian family. By abolishing private ownership, the Russian Revolution brought a sexual revolution in its wake. The family and established morality disappeared in the immense social upheaval. The new Soviet legislation reflected this evolution—marriage and divorce became simple formalities; sexual relationships between young people were allowed and took place; abortion was legal and free; and everyone could buy contraceptives for a few kopecks.

When the bureaucratic Stalinist rule began, they hastened to put an end to the sexual revolution. Puritan concepts had always prevailed in the heart

[9]*The Sexual Struggle of Youth,* pp. 89–90.

of the Bolshevik party (Lenin was very conservative in this regard). At first, voices were raised against the young people's "abandon" and the "dissolute life" they led. Bourgeois influences were held responsible for their "unrestrained sensuality." Toward the middle of the thirties, laws punishing homosexuality and forbidding abortion were passed. The cult of the family made its appearance in the USSR and enjoyed a vogue which in no way differed from that instituted by the Nazis. The official moral code could have been confused with middle-class morality in capitalist countries, and a burdensome conformity finally colored everyday life.

In *The Sexual Revolution,* Reich offers a brilliant study of the decline of sexual freedom in the USSR, where the reappearance of sexual repression and of the patriarchal family confirmed his theories on the social role and historical origin of sexual repression.

Chapter X

Criticism of Psychoanalysis

We have seen that Freud considered infantile sexual repression to be an indispensable stage along the road leading to the socialization of the individual; for this in effect facilitates the repression of genital needs in the adult. Now, according to Freud, the renunciation of these needs is a necessary condition for the continued existence of civilization and culture. Again according to Freud, a civilization can only prosper if the people repress their sexuality and devote themselves to more worthwhile activities. Freud had advanced the theory of sublimation to justify the sexual privations that society expects of its members. Sublimation is then a process by which the libido (sexual energy) converts itself into work energy. Having observed the effect that sexual repression has on the organism, Reich rejected the Freudian theory of sublimation. Reich agreed with Freud in one respect: our society could not survive for long if people did not repress their sexual needs. In effect, the foundations of society are built on sexual repression. But sexual repression does not increase people's capacity for work; it makes them docile and prepares them to accept the established order. Parents repress their children's sexuality to bring them to order, helping to ensure the cohesion of the family cell. The family is a state in miniature in which the child learns to obey and to restrain his rebellious instincts. Given that the state needs the family as a means of education and that family unity requires children and parents to repress their sexual needs, sexual repression definitely succeeds in perpetuating the state.

A good illustration of this mechanism can be seen in the reinstatement of the family in the USSR. When the regime began to crystallize and a ruling class made its appearance, they began to paste together the broken shards of the family.

In *The Revolution Betrayed,* Trotsky writes:

> The most compelling motive of the present cult of the family is undoubtedly the need of the bureaucracy for a stable hierarchy of relations, and for disciplining youth by means of 40,000,000 homes serving as points of support for authority and power.[1]

Having rejected the concept of sublimation, Reich refuted the Freudian interpretation of masochism and sadism. In Chapter V, I tried to show how Freud arrived at his explanation for the existence of a death instinct in human beings, and how destructive behavior, sadism, and masochism, can be looked at in terms of the death instinct. Masochism was the direct expression of this instinct. Sadism resulted from a joining of the sexual instinct and the destructive instinct focused on an exterior object. Freud also attributed the obstinacy with which pa-

---

[1]Doubleday, Doran & Co., 1937, p. 153.

tients clung to their sickness and the reason for the unexpected recurrence of certain neuroses, to the compulsion to repeat.

Reich rejected the idea of the death instinct because it seemed to him to be a gratuitous and arbitrary construction. Even if the existence of a sexual instinct can be inferred from sexual behavior, cruelty and unkindness cannot necessarily be explained away by the existence of another instinct.

In 1932, Reich questioned the Freudian interpretation of masochism in an article published by the *International Journal of Psychoanalysis*. There is a story behind the publication of this article. Freud, as director of the *Journal,* wanted to precede the article with a note warning the reader that Reich was a Communist and that his opinions reflected those of the Communist Party. The Berlin psychoanalysts protested and succeeded in getting Freud to withdraw his warning. Instead, a psychoanalyst by the name of Siegfried Bernfeld published an article in the same issue attacking Reich's contributions to Marxist sociology.

Reich started his article with an analysis of the masochistic character, whose dominant traits are a permanent sensation of suffering, expressed in perpetual lamentations and tales of woe; a tendency to underestimate himself and to present himself in a unfavorable light; a certain gaucheness in behavior and in human relations; and, finally, a marked propensity to provoke and torment those around him.

In analyzing these character traits, Reich found that they took the form of a challenge. The masochist is hoping to get other people to react to his continual complaints and tales of woe. He is not asking to be beaten precisely, but he is trying to make the people he is talking to lose their tempers so that he may reproach them for their unkindness toward him. By boring his friends, he finally succeeds in annoying them, giving himself an excuse to say, "See how you treat me. How mean you are to me. You're unkind and you don't like me." Beyond this provocation, says Reich, lies great self-deception and a considerable yearning for love. By looking hang-dog, the masochist is, in his way, begging for proof of love. A permanent and painful psychological tension grows out of his inability to appease his excessive need for affection. His feelings of suffering correspond to this tension of which he is unable to rid himself.

It was believed that the masochist sought out suffering because he enjoyed experiencing pain. Reich discovered that this was not so. The realization came to him in the following way: One day when he was overtaxed by a patient who was begging to be beaten, Reich lost patience and hit him. The patient cried out in pain, but gave no sign of pleasure. Reich concluded that his paradoxical behavior arose from an enormous anxiety associated with sexual feelings. When a masochist's desires go beyond a certain point, the guilt is so intense that the feelings become intolerable. He suffers from chronic frustration, and is prepared to go to any length to find release, but he wants others to assume the responsibility for his pleasure. For example, a woman with masochistic tendencies will make love imagining that she is being raped. The masochist's need for punishment has the following meaning:

. . . to bring about the relaxation after all, by way of a detour, and to shift the responsibility to the punishing person. We see the same mechanism in this basic process as in the characterological superstructure. In the latter it is: "Love me, so I won't be afraid"; the complaining means: "*You* are to blame, not I." The beating fantasy means: "Beat me, so I can get relaxation without being responsible for it."[2]

Reich maintains that the masochist's libido flows back to the anal stage, because anal pleasure is not very intense and does not go beyond the point at which anxiety appears. The way in which the masochist derives genital satisfaction demonstrates this. When he masturbates, for example, he defers ejaculation as long as possible because he finds the sudden rise of excitation to be an anxiety-producing experience. In brief, Reich concludes, the masochist is looking for pleasure like everyone else, but the fear of punishment interferes at the critical moment and makes him adopt aberrant behavior: "Hit me, so I can have sexual satisfaction and it will be your fault." The fantasy of being mistreated in a way forestalls the more serious punishment he fears.

Reich finished his article by saying that he had certainly not resolved all the problems of masochism, but that he hoped he had cleared a path for further studies by dismissing the hypothesis of a death instinct.

In the same article, he devoted a few lines to sadism. Behind sadistic character traits, he never discovered anything but sexual frustration. If a child is weaned too abruptly, one is stopping him from obtaining pleasure by sucking (the libido is at its oral stage), and he will later show destructive ten-

---

[2]*Character Analysis,* p. 243.

dencies. If one analyzes these tendencies, one finds that in the patient's mind they have assumed the meaning of biting the frustrating party. When the educators shorten the time that a child spends on his pot, they are depriving him of anal pleasure, and anal sadism will develop in the adult, characterized by the impulse to pulverize and crush. Finally, the repression of genital sexuality brings about the desire to pierce, and to penetrate (phallic sadism).

A mixture of destructive tendencies makes up these partial sadisms. Reich's theory can, then, be demonstrated by this illustration:

Frustration ———▶ agression

In rejecting the hypothesis of an instinct to suffer or to inflict suffering, Reich renounced the metaphysical explanations. It is very easy to say that a masochist, having once experienced pain, wishes to repeat this experience because of a "compulsion to repeat functioning beyond the pleasure principle." Just as Freud interpreted the repeated failures of neurotics, their tendency to commit the same mistakes continually as long as they live, as a compulsion to repeat, Reich held that this kind of blanket explanation unfortunately does not lead anywhere.

Sadism and masochism are then secondary impulses and not instincts. The distinction between primary impulses (biological) and secondary impulses (coming from the repression of instincts) is fundamental to Reich's thinking. Very often these secondary impulses have biological origins attributed to them, a mistake that Freud made. But Reich argues that everything cruel, aggressive, or perverse in man stems from the frustration of primary needs (hunger and the sexual instinct). Man is not born perverse. He becomes so when he is deprived of elemental satisfaction. Today, if the individual's unconscious contains impulses incompatible with life in society, it is the fault of patriarchal education and antisexual morality. Society itself engenders the asocial desires that it condemns. This means that by changing society, one could at the same time abolish the material conditions that make man a perverse and cruel animal.

Those who molest children are disturbed, and morality reproves this kind of behavior with good cause. But in a society where sexual freedom reigned, sadism or the temptation to abuse children would no longer exist, making superfluous the moral code that condemns these acts. Similarly, hunger induces people to steal, and theft leads to the repression of thieves. Do away with hunger, people will no longer steal, and there will be no more need of laws condemning thieves.

Reich therefore arrived at the conclusion that a healthy individual, that is, one who is orgastically potent, has no need to be kept on a leash by repressive morality. In effect, perverse impulses stem from the fixation of the libido at infantile phases and are fed by the sexual stasis. Since the libido of a healthy individual is entirely genital and is discharged regularly in the sexual act, he has no cruel tendency to repress. The healthy organism is then capable of autoregulation, that is to say he can go beyond an exterior authoritarian morality and behave spontaneously in a responsible fashion:

This is so because the energy is being withdrawn from the antisocial impulses; there is little left which needs to be kept under control. The healthy individual has no compulsive inhibition. What antisocial impulses may be left are easily controlled, provided the basic genital needs are satisfied.[3]

Reich created the expression *sex economy* to describe the way in which the libido is used by the organism; i.e., the relationship between the genital and pregenital libido, between the quantity of sexual energy released during the orgasm, and that which remains dammed up in the body.

For example, the libido can be totally fixed on the infantile stages of its development, creating a perverse or neurotic individual. Or it can be partially spent in the sexual act, the deficit being used to reactivate partial secondary impulses. A healthy sex economy means that the libido spends itself entirely in the sexual act.

Reich coined the term "sex economy" through an analogy with political economy. When one speaks of the economy of a country, one means the manner in which the country uses its resources, the distribution of investments to different branches of production, and so forth.

Reich still leveled considerable criticism at psychoanalysis. One example to which I have already referred was that of the Oedipus complex. To many psychoanalysts, this complex is a universal phenomenon, moreover it is reflected in the myths, legends, and institutions of primitive peoples; in ev-

---

[3] *The Sexual Revolution*, p. 6.

ery society, in every age, little boys have desired their mothers and detested their fathers. When faced with the Trobriand Islanders where no trace of the Oedipus complex, as described by Freud, can be found, the English psychiatrist Jones came up with a farfetched theory to prove that mother right and ignorance of paternity can be interpreted as an unconscious desire to repress the Oedipus complex even more deeply.

Among the Trobriand Islanders the child is brought up by his father and his maternal uncle. The latter represents the voice of authority and teaches the child discipline. The father is a friendly companion, and the Trobrianders do not recognize the role he played in the child's conception. A very strict taboo prohibits incestuous relations between brothers and sisters. Malinowski has ascertained that Trobrianders desire their sister and hate their maternal uncle (their mother's brother). These sentiments correspond to the Oedipus complex as it is known in our patrilineal society and are equally repressed. Therefore, incestuous love for the sister and hatred of the maternal uncle constitute the "family complex" in matrilineal societies. Jones did not accept Malinowski's view and wanted to prove at any price that an Oedipus complex was present in Trobriand families, but that it had been repressed and disguised. Thus, says Jones, the hatred that the son feels toward his father is transferred to his mother's brother, and the love for his mother is supplanted by love for his sister. Jones maintained that the Trobrianders' failure to recognize the relationship between the sexual act and procreation is an attempt to escape the hatred toward the father by ignoring his part in the reproduction process. In this way Jones managed to establish that the whole matriarchal system of the Trobrianders stemmed from a desire to obliterate the Oedipus complex. In the controversy between Jones and Malinowski, Reich obviously was on the anthropologist's side. The way in which Jones approached a sociological problem is typical of a psychoanalyst: he reverses the hierarchy of factors which condition behavior, and he ends up by explaining all the social structures in terms of the individual. For example, instead of seeing the child's feelings toward his parents as derived from a family structure determined by social and economic factors, psychoanalysts believe these feelings are hereditary and turn somersaults to prove that the matriarchal institutions of primitive people were formed in order to exorcise the Oedipus complex.

The psychoanalysts' tendency to explain sociology through the individual ends in erroneous interpretations of social phenomena which Marxists refer to as "idealism." Each time that psychoanalysis has tried to go outside its own territory and encroach upon the social sciences, it has tipped over into idealism, says Reich.

In an article titled "Dialectical Materialism and Psychoanalysis" (which appears in the book *The Sexual Crisis,* published in 1934 by the French Communist Party), Reich discusses the problem of the relationship between psychoanalysis and Marxism. He emphasizes the revolution Freud had accomplished in psychology and stresses the scientific nature of psychoanalysis. Although it has given place to idealist deviations, psychoanalysis contains a nucleus of irrefutable discoveries which can enrich Marxism. It has taken the mystery out of the belief that man is moved to act by noble and disinterested motives. Behind these honorable motives, psychoanalysts often discovered less noble motivations. By refuting the belief that disinterested ideals spur man into action, psychoanalysis extends the Marxist criticism of ideologies. When the nineteenth century bourgeoisie justified its rapine wars and colonial conquests in the name of civilization, financial interests obviously lay behind these honorable pretexts. Similarly, when an educator torments and terrorizes children "for their own good," it is easy to discern sadistic tendencies in his conduct. Reich developed the theory that Marxism and psychoanalysis are complementary. For example, he said, psychoanalysis can help to supply the missing elements of social psychology in Marxism. Naturally, some of Freud's assertions must be revised and placed in a sociological context. This holds true in particular for the reality principle: Freud would have us believe that the child learns to live in society by renouncing his pleasure and deferring satisfaction; that is by substituting the reality principle for the pleasure principle. To psychoanalysts the reality principle embraces all social constraints. Reich agrees with this but maintains that the reality principle reflects the demands of a class society and not those of an exterior abstract world. The reality principle is therefore relative. Reich had foreseen the growing respectability and acceptance of psychoanalysis for some time. He traced the development of psychoanalysis in a bourgeois society as follows:

> The tendency to compromise and capitulate before bourgeois sexual morality could be seen most clearly in the treatment of neuroses where

an eminently revolutionary theory was practiced on an individual who formed part of the capitalist society. The psychoanalyst's situation prohibited him from explaining frankly that today's sexual morality, marriage, the bourgeois family, and bourgeois education cannot be reconciled with a radical psychoanalytic cure of neuroses. We should openly admit that family conditions are distressing and that the sick person's environment is usually the greatest obstacle in the way of his cure; one is apprehensive—for reasons which are easily understood—to draw from these statements the conclusion they call for.[4]

After all, psychoanalysts are the children of the bourgeoise, and their patients for the most part come from the comfortable classes, which hardly disposes them to declare war on society.

---

[4]Translated from *The Sexual Crisis.*

Chapter XI

The Sexual Politics Association

When Reich arrived in Berlin in September 1930, he found the atmosphere far more favorable to his ideas than the psychoanalytic circles in Vienna had been; his orgasm theory and character analysis technique were warmly received. He made contact with the German Communist Party and became a member of the Communist cell called The Red Block, to which Arthur Koestler also belonged. The latter recalled Reich in his contribution to the book, *The God That Failed:*

Among other members of our cell I remember Dr. Wilhelm Reich, Founder and Director of *Sex-Pol* (Institute for Sexual Politics). He was a Freudian Marxist, inspired by Malinowski. He had just published a book called *The Function of the Orgasm,* in which he expounded the theory that the sexual frustration of the Proleteriat caused a thwarting of its political consciousness; only through a full, uninhibited release of the sexual urge could the working-class realize its revolutionary potentialities and historic mission; the whole thing was less cockeyed than it sounds. After the

150

victory of Hitler, Reich published a brilliant psychological study of the Nazi mentality, which the Party condemned; he broke with Communism and is now director of a scientific research institute in the U.S.A.[1]

In 1930, the German Communist Party was the most important in the capitalist world. It had 124,000 members and reaped 4,590,000 votes in the 1930 elections, as against 8,575,000 Socialist votes. That same year, Piatnitsky, the head of the Comintern secretariat (he was assassinated several years later in the USSR) wrote of the German Communist Party: "Among the network of Communist parties in capitalist countries, the first place belonged to and belongs to the German Communist Party. It is the best organized and the strongest in terms of numbers. It has put down deep roots into the working class and has the support of the masses."

The Weimar Republic was in ferment. Nazis, Socialists, and Communists fought for power. They not only confronted one another in parliament but also in armed struggles. The Berlin night was often torn by gunfire as the Nazis raided sections of the town held by the Communists, or vice versa.

If the Communists' electoral victories were appreciable, those of the Nazis were breathtaking; they rose from 800,000 votes in 1928 to 6,500,000 in 1930.

Reich got to know the Communist youth by attending their meetings. The principal problem of those in charge of these groups was to find the right terms on which to approach other young workers. They distributed tracts outside factories, made door-

[1]Bantam Books, 1967, p. 37.

to-door calls selling brochures, and painted slogans on walls, but to no avail. The recruitment did not noticeably increase, and the party functionaries were tearing their hair. For several months, Reich took part in the attempts to interest the people in the Party politics. Usually, he said, this took place on Sundays, even in good weather, and it called for considerable courage. They went from house to house offering their newspapers, and trying, if possible, to enter into conversation with those who came to the door. If they rang the bell of a Socialist or a Nazi, the door was slammed in their faces. In any case, sales were low; only the converted bought the German Communist Party's literature. Things hardly went any better in the country. Reich remembers that one day he was selected to explain to the peasants the advantages of the collectivization of land as it is practiced in the USSR—a subject he knew well since he had just returned from Russia. Several farmers asked him what would become of the Church if the Communists came to power, but other than that his speech was met by general indifference.

Party bureaucrats came to the young people's meetings to give lectures on Marxist doctrine or on economic subjects. Everyone had to make an effort to appear interested and not to fall asleep. Reich recalls an enormous meeting at the Berlin Sports Arena where twenty thousand workers and employees had come to hear Thälmann, the secretary of the German Communist Party. The feeling within the arena was electrifying until Thälmann climbed onto the platform and began an analysis of the state budget. In less than half an hour the atmosphere was Siberian.

Reich recounts numerous anecdotes of his life as a militant. In July 1931, a rumor ran through Berlin that the Nazis were planning to occupy the town. The German Communist Party mobilized its troops. Reich found himself at his cell headquarters together with about thirty comrades, both men and women. They had three revolvers at their disposal, but only four men knew how to use them. They hastily filled buckets of water and prepared to throw them at the Nazis, who, fortunately, did not appear.

At the beginning of 1931, Reich began to form an organization called the German Association for Proletarian Sexual Politics. He went about it in the same way as he had his centers of sexual hygiene in Vienna but with a different aim in view and with considerably more funds. In Vienna, Reich had tried to prevent neuroses and psychoses; he had come to realize, however, that this task was impossible in the present social context since neuroses and mental troubles are caused by family education and the family is an indispensable institution in a capitalist society at the same level as the state or the police. Therefore, Reich reasoned, capitalism must be overthrown. He resolved to fight it on the family level by influencing the sexual life of the young people. For in this way he would be attacking established sexual morality and undermining the family bases. The young people would learn to give in less readily to paternal authority, and prove less vulnerable to the conformist ideologies preached by their families. At the same time they would become more receptive to revolutionary propaganda.

Next, sexual needs are material needs, as imperious and concrete as hunger. In the same way that famine can trigger riots, if the proletariat were made aware of its sexual frustration it could be led to demand the legalization of abortion and the sale of contraceptive devices. The establishment of these measures would allow for more fluid sexual commerce, which would make the "taming" of the proletariat less easy to accomplish. (We should bear in mind that sexual repression causes the individual to fear freedom and submit readily to authority).

On the other hand, Reich was disgusted by the pornographic industry which exploited the sexual misery of the masses. The proliferation of pornographic films, newspapers, and reviews revealed the existence of a terrible sexual famine from which charlatans were profiting. In establishing his Sexual Politics Association, Reich hoped to remedy this situation, which, in return, would help to bring the "great day" closer.

At last, thought Reich, the time will come for the Communists to take the monopoly of sexual education away from the ruling classes. He stressed the part the Church plays in sowing the seeds of sexual guilt among young people by threatening them with the worst moral and physical torture, not to mention that super-Auschwitz beyond the clouds that is awaiting them if they "give in to their instincts." Priests are as guilty as the publishers of obscene magazines in poisoning sexuality. Reich often emphasized that one must fight against the Church's influence if one wishes to free sexuality. In any case, whether it is dispensed by adherents to a religion, or by laymen, sexual education is always carried out in a reactionary spirit. Whereas the Sexual Politics Association approached sexual questions in a progressive light linking the sexual emancipation of the proletariat to the Revolution.

In the thirties there were about eighty associations in Germany concerned with birth control and fighting for the legalization of abortion, etc., but they defended the family and marriage and for this reason they were not prepared to raise the question of adolescent sexual freedom. These associations had 350,000 members in all—more than any of the political parties.

Reich resolved to recruit some of them and proposed a platform of which the German Communist Party approved. He presented his program at a congress which was held in Düsseldorf in 1931; by the conclusion of the meeting, eight associations had joined Reich's program; and the 20,000 members that they represented made up the nucleus of The Sexual Politics Association. The movement spread swiftly and in a few months membership had doubled.

Reich then started to take the Communist youth in hand. The principal difficulty for young people was to find a sexual partner, although the boys were naturally more conscious of it than the girls. On many occasions during their meetings, they had asked if rooms could be made available to them so that they could make love. Reich gave them encouragement and the young people felt they had finally found someone who understood their problems and was concerned with the concrete realities of their everyday existence. Meanwhile Reich's relationship with the Communists was without a blemish. He became a familiar figure in the Berlin, Stettin, Dresden, and Leipzig factories as he traveled around, speaking at meetings, giving lectures, and organizing debates. The Sexual Politics Association grew and set up branches in the industrial centers of the Ruhr Valley. The Young Communists' cells came back to life, and their meetings swelled as word spread to the Hitler Youth and Catholic organizations that the "Reds" had a sympathetic doctor with whom one could discuss forbidden subjects.

Reich noticed a curious paradox: In the course of a debate on sexual problems, people spoke more freely than if they were alone with him. When he treated a patient individually, it took a long time before she felt sufficiently confident to discuss her problems frankly. On the other hand, when this same patient found herself in a group where the subject was being discussed collectively, she saw she was not alone in her situation and opened up more easily.

Reich wrote a number of little brochures addressed to parents and children where he gave simple and practical advice on sex education, sex life, and birth control. Like all growing organizations, The Sexual Politics Association needed more and more outlets. Reich spent a lot of time building it up. The movement became so large that finally the police were involved. The German Communist Party leaders also looked upon Reich's success with suspicion. He was not easy to handle and wasted no time in criticizing Party politics, which he considered to be too involved in parliamentary matters. Reich's growing influence over the young Communists began to cause the leaders of the German Communist Party some anxiety. The first sign of their discontent came with the troubles that beset his book *Der Sexuale Kampf der Jugend* (*The Sexual Struggle of Youth*).

Many people had asked Reich to write a book specifically for the young. He edited a manuscript which he circulated among the Party militants, asking them to give him their suggestions, criticisms, and comments. In light of these remarks, he rewrote the manuscript and submitted the final version to those in charge of the Communist youth. They approved it. But in order to obtain the final stamp of approval, the book still had to go to Moscow. The manuscript returned from Moscow accompanied by a favorable review and the curious suggestion that the workers' cultural organization should publish it rather than the German Communist Party press. They also insisted that Reich introduce certain modifications into the text. After a tight bargaining session, he made some corrections, but in the preface he took care to warn the reader that the book did not entirely reflect his opinions. Despite this, in March 1932 the book still had not appeared; whereupon Reich founded a publishing house (Sexpol Verlag) which immediately published *The Sexual Struggle of Youth*. Four thousand copies were sold in six weeks.

The Sexual Struggle of Youth is a short book which deserves some comment. I can find no work on sexual education to measure up to it. Reich approaches his subject in clear, simple, and direct language. His enormous experience shows through on every page. If he had not spent years dealing with the sexual problems of the working classes, he would never have been able to write this book. Here, for example, is how he explains to the young people the reason for the chastity which society imposes on them:

> In order to repress his sexual tendencies and desires the individual must use up a large amount of physical energy. This inhibits and injures the development of other activities, of reason, and of criticism. On the other hand, if sexuality is allowed to blossom in a healthy and vigorous fashion, one becomes free and active in the criticism of one's behavior in general. But this is precisely what capitalism cannot tolerate and why it rigorously defends authority and tradition. *The limitation of freedom of physical activity and criticism through sexual repression is one of the most important reasons for the bourgeois sexual order.* We can now understand why the bourgeoisie fight with all the means at its disposal to maintain and reinforce family morality. Because, as we have already said, the middle-class family is, above all, a factory turning out submissive beings.[2]

And Reich continues:

> Abstinence is insisted upon in a particularly severe fashion during puberty because in general it is precisely at this age that the youth begins to revolt against the family home. The sexual needs and strengths of each individual are raised against the oppressors. In all families, almost without exception, puberty is the time when the most bitter conflicts arise between parents and adolescents. In cases where the adolescent has not been entirely oppressed, as for example in small tradesmen's and employees' families, he begins to revolt more and more against the obligation to spend beautiful

[2]*Op. cit.*

Sunday afternoons in the company of adults at an inn, listening to boring conversations. Sooner or later, each adolescent begins to catch a more or less clear glimpse of the fact that his place is elsewhere, with other adolescents; that he is bored around adults; that he wants air, sunshine, physical education, and sexual intercourse.[3]

In the first chapter, titled "Reproduction," Reich gives a summary of the anatomy and physiology of the genital system; he explains in detail how to use contraceptives and how to get hold of them. He also devotes a paragraph to abortion and explains why there are laws prohibiting it.

In the chapter called "Sexual Tension and Satisfaction," Reich describes the sexual act with the help of several illustrations which show the mounting excitation and its abrupt fall with the orgasm. He reviews all the troubles that can affect sexual intercourse (impotence, frigidity, insufficient pleasure, etc.) and gives advice on remedying them. In short he touches on every aspect of sexuality which might preoccupy young people, including homosexuality and masturbation.

The book closes with these lines:

We have proof that socialism alone can bring about sexual freedom. That is why in a capitalist society we must use all our strength to convince the millions of oppressed that our view is correct and to mobilize them in the relentless fight against everyone who is opposed to their liberation. The youth will march among the first ranks of this assembly because of the great material, authoritarian, and sexual oppression

---

[3]*Ibid.*

which they suffer, and which unite all young people. We shall win over all the young people and fire them with enthusiasm for the revolutionary cause because we alone understand their sexual misery, and we shall persuade them that the only thing we can say to them today, responsibly and in all good faith, is this: "There is no sexual liberation for youth under capitalism, no healthy and satisfying sexual life; if you want to do away with sexual misery, fight for socialism. Because socialism allows sexual satisfaction by ignoring those who have no clear opinions on sexual questions, and its first task is to do away with the domination of people who turn their eyes heavenwards when they mention love, and who, in reality, are destroying the youth's sexuality."[4]

In 1932, Reich still believed that socialism was taking hold in the USSR. Be that as it may, if one takes the word "socialism" in its original sense, which has nothing to do with the caricature of it that we see in Eastern countries today, Reich's conclusion remains valid, in the sense that the struggle for sexual freedom must be conducted on the same front as the fight against capitalism.

In December 1932 the Communists forbade the distribution of Reich's books through the youth movements. The representatives of the Sexual Politics Association demanded an explanation and sought out the dignitaries of the German Communist Party; a Berlin subsidiary of the Association went so far as to demand the resignation of the leaders of the Party's cultural organization. The affair rapidly grew more vicious. The Communists

[4]*Ibid.*

maintained that Reich was "influencing their youth" and that the young people no longer docilely carried out the instructions that came from higher up. However, since there were no real charges against him, and his exclusion from the Party might cause a backlash among his many followers, the Communists realized the troublesome Dr. Reich could not be dropped then and there without a more concrete excuse.

The German Communist Party's sudden turnabout on the subject of Reich is explained by the political climate of the time. Reich was a revolutionary and by 1930, the European Communist parties shied from the possibility of revolution. When Lenin and Trotsky originally seized power in the USSR they put all their hopes in a general European revolution, for the idea of establishing socialism in a single country, and a country as little industrialized as Russia into the bargain, did not seem feasible. Unfortunately, their hope that the European proletariat would rise to its feet and overcome the bourgeoisie was not realized. Russia stood alone and had to get by under its own steam. Far from wasting away, the Soviet State reinforced itself. An even more encroaching and far-reaching bureaucracy was formed and consolidated its power. By 1932 this process was already very well advanced and the leaders in the USSR no longer wished for a worldwide revolution. In effect, the bureaucracy became a ruling class like any other, and its authority would have inevitably been questioned in the course of a European revolution. By one of those frequent turnabouts in history, the interests of a ruling class had been turned against them.

In the meantime, the European Communist

parties had become instruments in the service of the Kremlin's foreign policy. One of their duties was to snuff out all movements that looked as if they ran the risk of becoming revolutionary. Besides, the interests of the Russian bureaucracy were the same as those of the Communist parties; the latter were so rigid in their hierarchy that a revolution would have made them fall apart.

To get back to Reich, in good faith he believed, along with thousands of intellectual Germans, that the German Communist Party had the interests of the working classes at heart and was preparing for the Revolution. It was only after he had separated from the Communists in 1933 that he became fully aware of their conservative nature.

In 1933, his position within the German Communist Party became untenable, and Reich found he was losing a lot of time defending himself against his enemies within the Party. The functionaries never missed an opportunity to frustrate his projects. The German Communist Party press, which had earlier recommended the distribution of Reich's brochures, began to criticize them and advise the readers against them; they were enraged to discover that the youth cells had made it known they would continue to distribute Reich's brochures. In addition, Socialist and Communist workers had been fraternizing, contrary to the instructions of the Communist party leaders, who considered the Socialists to be "social Fascists." Reich had attempted to foster these spontaneous alliances, and at the request of a recently formed union of Socialist and Communist workers wrote a tract of which thousands of copies were distributed. He joined an armed group to fight the Nazis; once again this group was made up of

163 / The Sexual Politics Association

Socialists and Communists. As the March elections of 1933 approached, the electoral campaign began to look like guerrilla warfare. Reich could not understand why the German Communist Party would not join the Socialists, and he asked this question aloud causing the Party directors to accuse him of insubordination. In short, tension was mounting and the rupture was not far off.

The Nazi accession to power in 1933 put an end to the conflict by annihilating the German Communist Party. Reich slipped through the net and sought refuge abroad.

Chapter XII

Nazism

Reich first encountered Nazism in 1930 when he arrived in Berlin. Despite the success of the National Socialist Party, the Communists persisted in viewing Hitler as a mere agitator without a future and predicted a rapid Nazi decline. Reich did not share their point of view. The mass demonstrations organized by the Nazis, their publicity campaigns, which were remarkably orchestrated by Goebbels, and certain penetrating themes in Hitler's propaganda made him think that an unrecognized phenomenon was developing in Germany.

He watched their marches through Berlin, regularly read Nazi newspapers, studied their propaganda, analyzed the contents of Hitler's *Mein Kampf* and the works of the Nazi philosopher Alfred Rosenberg. He took notes, established statistics and accumulated documents. As his knowledge grew, he became aware of the gravity of the sickness that had struck Germany. Yet if he unburdened himself to the German Communist Party leaders and tried to make them understand that the Nazis represented a danger that must be taken seriously, they jeered at his fears, calling him an alarmist. Reich was still convinced that he was right and that his comrades understood nothing about Nazism. He even feared that the working classes would be seduced by Nazi propaganda one day, but when he voiced this opinion, his comrades scolded him to such an extent that he avoided bringing the subject up again. However, said Reich, one had only to attend a Nazi demonstration to see that a considerable percentage of the proletariat was involved. But he kept these reflections to himself, and began to write *Die Massenpsychologie Des Faschismus (The Mass Psychology of Fascism)*.

When discussing the phenomenon of Nazism, we must consider the whole series of economic, social, and historical factors which partially explain the birth and rise of Fascism in Germany.

For example, there is the Treaty of Versailles, imposed on the Germans by the victors of World War I. The French and English had agreed to divide up Germany's colonies; carry off her merchant navy; and try to exact enormous war reparations from her. (The financial debacle that Germany suffered after the defeat made it impossible for this latter clause to be realized; France retaliated by sending her army to occupy the Ruhr Valley). In addition, France had taken over the coal fields in the Saar; occupied the left bank of the Rhine; and obtained a guarantee that the German Army would not number more than 100,000 men. Finally, Germany had been forced to give up part of its territory to Poland; and the port at Danzig became a free port. The Germans obviously felt that they had been wronged, which explains their desire for revenge.

Another explanation for Hitler's rise is that the German capitalists feared the worker movement. In 1930, the heavy industry bosses began to subsidize the Nazi Party because they saw it as a defense against Communism.

Last but not least, Germany was hard hit by the Depression. The production index (1928 = 100) had sunk to sixty by the end of 1931. There were more than seven million unemployed. German factories were operating at fifty percent of their capacity. Foundry production fell from thirteen million tons to three million. The production crisis was augmented by a financial recession which forced the German capitalists to ask the state for help. But for many reasons the German statesmen would not listen to their demands, and the industrial magnates then turned to Hitler, this energetic man, and supported his drive for power.

All these factors are of importance; they are even essential in understanding Hitler's rise. But how the people became Nazi, and why German Imperialism took such an apocalyptic turn remains to be explained.

The spread of a political doctrine among the masses is like an epidemic; when a virus spreads through a population, a certain degree of adaptation exists between the pathogenic agent and the individuals it contaminates. On the other hand, if the population has been immunized, there is no epidemic. In the case of Nazism, Reich determined to understand why the Germans were vulnerable to Nazi propaganda. He undertook a concrete analysis of the propaganda, as well as the sociological and psychological characteristics of the classes where it took hold most easily.

The Nazis began by concentrating on the middle

classes, this heterogeneous mixture of employees, small tradesmen, and blue-collar workers.

The middle classes in Germany had not stopped deteriorating since 1918. The collapse of the mark had ruined the stockholders and investors; while the creation of big department stores drove the little storekeepers into bankruptcy; and industrial concentration made life hard for small contractors. The impoverished middle class was thus slipping backwards toward the proletariat. The idea of finding itself on a level with the proletariat horrified the middle class. A white-collar worker would consider becoming a factory worker, a fate of the worst sort. A ruined grocer will cling to his counter rather than beat a retreat to the factory. It is hard to understand why the discontented middle classes were not amenable to Socialism. Reich explains that it is because they are situated between the bourgeoisie and the proletariat and hold fast to their few privileges. They consider themselves above the working classes; any declaration against private ownership is a threat to them. As long as the small shopowner does a minimal trade, he will hang on to it over and above everything, even if he is earning less than a skilled worker.

Secondly, the rivalry between small tradesmen hinders the growth of class solidarity and encourages individualist attitudes of the "each man for himself" kind. Finally, bureaucrats tend to "identify" with the authority of the state; that is, to adopt the characteristics and attitudes of another more prestigious person. Functionaries, says Reich, submit to the authority of the state at the same time as they represent it, behaving like flunkies who have acquired their masters' habits.

This identification with authority is frequently found among the petit bourgeoisie. When a typist talks of the company where she is employed by saying "we," she is identifying with the company bosses. Evidently this attitude stands in the way of progressive initiative. How can the employees be made to understand that they are being exploited and that their interests are those of the proletariat, if they slavishly copy their superiors and feel that they belong to an elite? Thus, even on the brink of ruin, and fearing that they were being drawn down into the proletarian class, the petit bourgeoisie was in revolt and open to the anti-capitalist sentiments expressed by Nazi propaganda:

> Without his promise to fight big business, Hitler never would have won over the middle class strata. They carried him to victory because they were against big business. Under their pressure, the Nazis had to institute anti-capitalistic measures, just as under the pressure of big business they had to scrap them again.[1]

Nazi propaganda did then have revolutionary accents; not sufficiently socialist to scare off the petit bourgeoisie, but enough to attract them. Reich stresses the two-facedness of Nazism:

> Insofar as National Socialism had to emphasize its middle class character (before the seizure of power and immediately afterwards) it was in fact *anti-capitalistic and revolutionary*. Insofar as (for the solidification and maintenance of its regime) it shed its anti-capitalistic character more and more and showed its capitalistic func-

---

[1] Wilhelm Reich, *The Mass Psychology of Fascism* (Orgone Institute Press, 1946), p. 35.

tion more and more exclusively, it became the extreme defender of imperialism and the capitalist economic order.[2]

Although the petit bourgeoisie is not a determining factor in history, it can certainly influence the course of events at given periods, as the fact that it served as a springboard for Hitler proves.

One of the most obsessive themes of Hitler's propaganda dealt with the Jews, presented as Germany's number one enemy. The tactic of finding a scapegoat for all the difficulties that assail a community has often been used by dictators, and Hitler was no exception. The Nazis accused the Jews of polluting German blood, of weakening the race, of destroying morality, and of exploiting the country. Making the Jew the personification of capitalism, says Reich, is a cunning way of turning the feeling of the masses against the exploitative classes, while at the same time reassuring the latter. But antisemitic propaganda went much further than this. A newspaper called *Der Stürmer,* run by a psychopath named Julius Streicher, was dedicated entirely to antisemitism. It carried accounts of rapes and ritual murders committed by the Jews; the cartoons showed evil-looking Jews armed with knives, preparing to rape or slit young girls' throats. Although Reich knew how easily this approach can be analyzed, he felt it a waste of time to talk to a Nazi and attempt to show him that it is the product of a sick mind. It is more important to understand why *he* has been hypnotized by these stories.

The statement that Jews pollute the German blood, says Reich, plays on the fear of venereal dis-

---

[2]*Ibid.,* pp. 35–36.

ease. This fear is buried deep in the collective unconscious as a result of the antisexual terrorism practiced by priests against young people. "Sexual relationships are a mortal sin punished by disease." To accuse the Jews of defiling the blood and the race is thus tantamount to accusing them of spreading syphilis.

On the other hand, the Nazis presented the Jews as a menace to the strength and virility of the Aryans. If one considers these statements in the light of the cartoons where Jews are depicted armed with knives, continues Reich, the meaning of all this becomes clear. Jews castrate the Aryans and lust after their women. Here we are no longer dealing with the fear of syphilis, but the fear of castration. The fact that the Jews circumcise their sons adds to the irrational fear that they inspire as castrators. In sum, German antisemitism stemmed from a hatred of capitalists carried over to the Jews, from a castration complex, and from the fear of venereal diseases.

Finally, Nazi propaganda accused the Jews of being disruptive agents, undermining the morality and traditional culture of the Northern peoples. Behind this obscure threat of social chaos lay the fear that the forces that are boiling up within the unconscious would be liberated and civilization would fall apart. The petit bourgeoisie has an instinctive aversion to disorder, which can be explained by their life style. They lead a bleak, tight existence and as a reaction adopt a strict moral code, dictated by honor and duty. Obedience, respect for the social order, and the need to save money are buried deep in their mentality. Obliged to justify his condition, the petit bourgeois has made a virtue of necessity. Furthermore, his morality is rooted in a particular family structure. Of all the social classes, the middle classes are those where family ties are the most restricting and where sexual life is the most repressed. The need to keep a close check on the sexuality of women and young girls makes for an even more obsessive morality, and the sexual repression is more intense. Thus, the thought of social disorder and a weakening of the moral code arouses the fear of the perverse impulses which are fermenting in the petit bourgeois unconscious.

The influence of the authoritarian family has repercussions at other levels too; besides an identification with the strict father, we find a strong mother fixation, that is, in effect, an umbilical cord continues to bind the son to his mother. The son cannot break away; he shows that he is unable to form new relationships and never becomes truly adult. Identification with the father and a mother fixation stand in the way of the individual's escape from the family circle, which is seen, though not necessarily consciously, as a close attachment to the family. Fixation to the family circle is a forerunner of nationalistic attitudes, to the extent that the Motherland is identified with the mother and family home.

The Nazi philosopher Rosenberg continually refers to the idea that racial interbreeding leads to the degeneration of the race. The Nazis employed this theme abundantly. Sifting through the arguments that Rosenberg used to justify his thesis, Reich came to the conclusion that the idea that interbreeding leads to the decline of the race is due in part to the petit bourgeois' fear of seeing their authoritarian morality, their values and social privileges absorbed into the proletariat. In effect, the petit bourgeois had pulled himself up to an intermediary level between the bourgeoisie and the proletariat through hard work and saving. Thus, the fear of seeing his children marrying into the working class is very much alive for him. When the daughter of a government employee asks if she may marry a member of the proletariat, her parents nearly have heart attacks. The interbreeding taboo therefore means: "No marriage with members of the lower classes." Race has taken on the meaning of class, and interbreeding means marrying beneath one's station.

Hitler's charisma, his popularity and influence were irrational factors that only a psychoanalyst could understand.

The family and the school manufacture disciplined robots, trained to obey and in need of direction. A population conditioned in this way will easily give up its independence to a political pirate, especially if he puts himself across as a messiah whose task is to save the nation.

Those who are afraid of liberty are prepared to give themselves to a wonderful leader because it is so comforting to put one's destiny in the hands of such a man. One no longer has to accept responsibility, and one waits for the solution to all one's problems to descend from the heavens. Hitler, surrounded by a mystical halo, fit this image perfectly. He did not waste his time arguing but hammered at his listeners with speeches that set the chords of their collective unconscious vibrating. He had exceptional gifts as an orator, and played on an irrational register—the chauvinism and inferiority complex of the Germans, their need for domination and for revolt.

Hitler promised the women that he would relegate them to the position of broody hens. They voted for him en masse because the idea of sexual liberty deeply alarms those who have interiorized their sexual repressions. He founded the cult of the family, of the Fatherland, and of the state. He enrolled the youth in para-military organizations and instilled in them the sense of martial values. When they played at war, the boys could take themselves seriously.

Hitler promised the Germans that he would wipe out the terms of the Versailles Treaty and that their country would become the most powerful in the world. He undertook to abolish the proletarian condition, dissolving the class system in the melting pot of a revived nation. There would be no more proletarians, no more bourgeois, but there would be Germans. His racial theory, according to which mankind is divided into superior and inferior races, appealed to the man in the street. The last little shopkeeper could say to himself that he belonged to a race of superior beings and identify with his Führer. He made revolutionary speeches to the proletariat and spoke reassuringly to the capitalists. He took everyone in with diabolical ease. His doctrine may be a hotchpotch of contradictions, but it was adapted to the psychology of the masses, because this psychology is molded from pathological elements engendered by sexual repression and authoritarian education. Hitler's success depended entirely on the character structure of the masses.

When several political parties are vying for an electorate, the competition is governed by laws identical to those of natural selection in biology. The electoral growth of one party indicates that its ideology caters to a collective need and is adapted to the social conditions of the day. On the other hand, if the membership of another party remains for a long period of time in the region of three percent of the total electorate, this party has no chance of rallying the masses, unless a change in the economic situation modifies the social picture.

Reich analyzed the Nazi phenomenon by dissecting the collective mentality of the Germans, and he showed that Hitler's doctrine fit it most snugly. This enabled him to predict in 1933 that a worldwide catastrophe was in the making. He knew the irrational depths of human nature and had recognized that Hitler was aiming all his propaganda at them. But one would search Reich's work in vain to find the least sign of hatred or suspicion of the German people. He thought of Nazism as a collective neurosis, a phenomenon which could arise anywhere as long as the circumstances were ripe.

Chapter XIII

The Beginning of Exile

On February 24, 1933, Reich made a quick trip to Copenhagen where students had invited him to give a lecture on racism and Fascism. He returned to Berlin four days later, the night after the Reichstag had been burnt. This event had given the Nazis a pretext to suspend the constitutional rights of the people; and a wave of repression followed, in the course of which they disposed of their opponents by throwing them in jail.

Reich sent his children to Vienna and went to stay in a hotel under an assumed name. He recalls the terrible confusion of the following weeks; the Party's strength had been completely undermined and its nervous system paralyzed; some members were in prison, and others in flight; it was impossible to know where anyone was. Those who were in possession of firearms or who distributed tracts risked the death penalty. Two close friends of Reich, workers, were beaten up by the Nazis. On March 1, some young people came to borrow Reich's car to transport tracts and arms. If they were apprehended, they would pretend they had stolen the car, and

Reich was to protest that his car had disappeared if they had not returned by a certain hour. After their departure, Reich realized that they had forgotten to agree upon the street from which the car had supposedly been stolen. If they were caught and if he were confronted with them, they would all be in the soup. Hours passed and they did not return. Reich could no longer turn up at the police station to lodge his complaint. He thought of crossing the border that very night, but he had neither money nor a passport. His home had been visited by the Nazis and was under observation. Finally his friends returned very late. They had had a blowout.

The next day the *Volkischer Beobachter,* the Nazi party organ, attacked his book *The Sexual Struggle of Youth.* Reich could definitely no longer stay in Berlin. He decided to leave for Austria by train with his wife, alight before the frontier, and wait a few days in a little Bavarian town to see which way the wind was blowing. Despite the alarming news which reached him there from Berlin, he returned to the German capital and went to a hotel where he registered under his own name, reasoning it was the best way of escaping recognition. He learned that the Nazis had searched his home a second time. For several days he tried to get in touch with his comrades, but everyone was hiding. In the end he borrowed some money and made his way back to Vienna, leaving everything behind him.

In Vienna, Reich had to build up a practice from scratch. His reputation as a terrorist and Bolshevik did little to attract patients. His volatile temperament and the scathing tone he used in his polemics widened the gap between him and the other psychoanalysts with whom he had already been on bad terms when he left three years earlier. Since then, the Psychoanalytic Association had become a venerable institution and lost the pioneering spirit of Freud and his early disciples. After a lengthy struggle against silence and calumny, psychoanalysis was accepted by society and had become respectable. In view of these recent developments, Reich's return to Vienna was like a dog blundering into a game of ninepins. He repeated his criticism of the internal contradictions in psychoanalysis and warned his colleagues that by refusing to engage in the fight against Fascism they were putting a noose around their own necks. They treated him as an alarmist and a Communist fanatic, for they wanted to keep their science separate from politics, and the Psychoanalytic Association had already taken steps to ensure it would not be involved. In Berlin in October 1932, Eitingen, the president of the German Psychoanalytic Society, had already put several obstacles in Reich's path because he was marked politically. But this had not stopped many young analysts from attending his course on character analysis and the function of the orgasm. In January 1933, he had signed a contract with the International Psychoanalytic publishing house, which was to have published his book *Die Charakteranalyse*. But later in Vienna he was informed that, because of the political situation in Germany, it was impossible to publish a book written by a notorious Communist. Reich published the book at his own expense. The psychoanalysts' fear that they would be compromised in the political struggles began to seriously get on Reich's nerves. Several days after he gave a lecture to some socialist students, he received a letter from the president of the Association telling him not to address Communist or socialist gatherings again. Reich refused to comply with this demand. He was then told not to attend the meetings of the Association. Reich asked the Association's executive committee to meet with him for an open and frank discussion. During the meeting, which took place on April 21, 1933, Reich made the following proposition: He would abstain from publishing articles in the psychoanalytic reviews and would give up teaching classes in psychoanalysis, if the Association would officially announce the incompatibility between his psychoanalytic theories and his position as a member of the Psychoanalytic Association. He was never given a reply.

Disagreeable rumors reached his ears. A young Danish doctor who had come to serve an apprenticeship with Reich told him that the psychoanalysts had advised him against following Reich's courses because he was a Marxist. Finding this atmosphere unpleasant, Reich accepted an invitation to go to Copenhagen and train psychoanalysts. He left for Denmark at the end of April and arrived on May 1.

His first concern was to see his book *The Mass Psychology of Fascism* published. After considerable financial difficulties, the book appeared in August, and met with a warm reception; many copies were smuggled into Germany. Reich claimed that the working classes had suffered a serious defeat in allowing Hitler to take power; the Communists, unable to admit that this was so, condemned the book. According to them, the success of the Nazis was just a momentary flash and the German worker movement was progressing in spite of everything.

The Danish Communists went as far as to exclude Reich from their meetings. This was truly extraordinary since he was not a member of their Party.

It was not with a light heart that Reich severed his ties with the Communists. He recognized that after fighting alongside them for six years, they had become his only country. But once he was convinced of their treachery, he did not hesitate to fight against them, although the awareness was painful to him because it cast doubt on many things that he had taken to be true without a second thought. But it also proved fruitful, for he began to reflect on the role of political parties and on the evolution of the Soviet regime. Unlike many disappointed Communists, he was never attracted by Trotskyism. He only felt suspicious of the Trotskyites, who were trying to get a "new revolutionary party" on its feet to guide the masses toward socialism. The Trotskyite strategy of attempting to mould all the organizations into which they succeeded in infiltrating, seemed to him puerile and headed for disaster, and he rejected the overtures they made to him. At the end of the year 1933, Reich was compelled to leave Denmark. He had angered the Minister of Justice, who brought an action against the editor of the *Danish Communist Review* because he had published an article by Reich. (The editor was sentenced to forty days in jail). Thus, when Reich requested that his visitor's permit be renewed, he was refused.

Reich decided to emigrate to Sweden, the closest country to Denmark. But first he made a trip to London, where he met Malinowski for the first time. The two men hit it off right away. On the other hand, the English psychoanalysts were cool to him. He paid a visit to Jones, the president of the Psychoanalytic Association, knowing full well that their scientific positions were diametrically opposed since Jones looked upon the family and the Oedipus complex as biological phenomena. He had argued with Malinowski on this point some ten years earlier. Reich's interests were beginning to focus in the biological area. In Copenhagen he had already contemplated conducting laboratory experiments on the orgasm. He profited by his trip to London to consult a physiologist and ask him how one could measure the electric charges from the skin. If one is to believe Reich, the physiologist replied that it was impossible.

Reich left London and went to Paris where he met some German Trotskyites who had read *The Mass Psychology of Fascism* and agreed with his conclusions. They tried to enroll him in their group, but Reich would not allow himself to be recruited. Having attended some of their meetings, he grew tired of their dogmatism and turned away from them. After one particular meeting where they had discussed the role of the avant-garde and class consciousness, he returned to his hotel and outlined the plan for a brochure which he wrote in the Tyrol two weeks later. This brochure titled "What Is Class Consciousness?" appeared under the pseudonym of Ernst Parell in 1934.

After a detour to Swiss Germany where he met some sexologists, Reich finally rejoined his wife and children in the Tyrol. He spent the vacation with them, and left for Prague where the editorial staff of the *Weltbühne,* the intellectual leftist German paper, had found refuge. This paper had commented favorably on his book about Fascism. Instead of going on to Sweden via Poland, Reich decided to cross

Germany saying that he wanted to go by Berlin to avoid the long journey through Poland. His friends tried without success to dissuade him. Probably he already sensed that from now on his life would be spent in exile and he felt the need to see once more the country where he had fought for three years in the worker movement, and where his ideas had finally met with a real audience—the young workers. In 1945, when Germany had been crushed by bombs, Reich still thought of the friends he had lost.

Before he left, he inquired into the German police control methods and learned that their customs officials did not have complete lists of wanted persons.

In Berlin he had three hours before catching his connection to Scandinavia. He went for a walk through the familiar streets and was oppressed by the militarist atmosphere which weighed on the town. As he was boarding his train, a man on the platform stared at him. Reich felt that he had seen him before, but he did not even dare acknowledge him. Everyone was suspicious of everyone else. From one day to the next, hundreds of Communists turned to Fascism. Even the Communist workers were enrolling in the Nazi party; after the discipline the Communist Party had demanded of them, they were well prepared to become Nazis. Reich arrived in Sweden and settled in Malmö, where he lived with his friend Elsa Lindenberg. He was divorced.

Malmö is a little town situated in southern Sweden just across from Copenhagen. Reich describes it as a provincial city where malicious gossip is part of the daily conversation and where boredom breeds Fascism. In the evening, the young people strolled through the streets in little groups, the boys ogling the girls without daring to approach them.

Reich lived with Elsa Lindenberg in a dreary boarding house whose inhabitants were snobbish gentlemen wearing monocles and ladies of uncertain age. They gulped down their meals hurriedly and spent their time away from their lodgings. Each week Reich received a number of Danish students (Malmö is an hour from Denmark by ship) to whom he taught psychoanalysis. This coming and going finally attracted the attention of the idle police chief, who discreetly made inquiries into Reich's activities. When Reich realized that he was being followed, he pretended not to have noticed.

His students were requested to go down to the police station where they were questioned about him. They replied that he was a doctor and that they went to him to study psychoanalysis. The police chief, who was probably hearing the word "psychoanalysis" for the first time, suspected some devious political machinations and summoned Reich. Reich went to the police station and had a brief, unmannerly interview with the police. A few days later, the police conducted a search at his house. He was in the middle of typing a manuscript; after reading a few lines they gave up and began to ferret around. When Reich discovered they did not have a search warrant, he threw them out.

His request for an extension to his visitor's permit was refused and he was told to leave Sweden before May 24 or risk expulsion. He was very upset and obtained an extension to the ruling, which gave him time to prepare his departure in comfort. On June 4, he left Sweden and returned to Denmark, living there for several months under the assumed name of Peter Stein since he had been refused a visitor's permit in his own right.

In August 1934, the International Psychoanalytic Association held a congress in Lucerne. Reich arrived on August 25. The day before the congress was scheduled to start, the secretary of the Psychoanalytic Association took him to one side and informed him that he had been excluded from their circle, he was no longer authorized to participate in the work of the congress nor to read the paper he had prepared. Reich had not expected such a blow and demanded to know who had made this decision and why he had not been warned. He finally found out that the German Psychoanalytic Society had struck him off their list a year earlier and that the International Association had jumped at this opportunity to exclude him permanently. He was less surprised by the fact that he had been expelled than by the underhand way in which it had been carried out. Since the formulation of his orgasm theory some ten years earlier, he had been in constant conflict with his colleagues. His theories questioning the validity of the family, the state, and capitalism in general, disturbed the psychoanalysts who had been part of the system for some time now.

He had expected to be excluded one day or the next. He obtained permission from Jones to read his paper as a guest at the Conference, starting with these words:

"Having been a member of your Association for fourteen years, I am now addressing you as a guest."

While he spoke to the unreceptive audience, an idea flashed through his mind like lightning. He had the impression that he was assuming Freud's destiny, by developing, in the face of all opposition, the subversive ideas that the latter had expressed a very long time before at the beginning of his career. With a heavy heart Reich left Lucerne and returned to Denmark. He spent a few days in Copenhagen, time enough to get his things together, then left for Oslo. Since he was forbidden entry into Sweden, he had trouble at the border. Finally, after sending numerous telegrams, he was given permission to cross the country in order to get to Norway.

He spent five years in Oslo sinking into madness.

Chapter XIV

In Pursuit of the Libido

Reich's life falls into two distinct periods. The first ran from 1897 to 1934, and the second from 1934 to 1957, the year of his death.

In 1922, Reich began an outstanding career. He was probably the most brilliant second generation psychoanalyst—those who came after the War, who succeeded the great founders like Freud, Ferenczi, Abraham, etc., are considered second generation analysts—and became one of the best practitioners in Vienna.

However, while psychoanalysis was turning to the right, instead of falling into step with the rest of his colleagues, Reich turned toward the left and joined the Communist camp. When they, in their turn, helmed to the right, Reich found himself standing alone.

Meanwhile, he had accomplished an enormous amount of work. He had trained young therapists in the technical seminar he directed; he had formulated his orgasm theory and launched a new, empirical and hazardous therapeutic technique which considerably advanced psychoanalysis. In addition, he worked on a synthesis of Marxism and psychoanalysis, thereby moving in the direction advocated by Marx and Engels, who had always stressed the scientific nature of dialectical materialism and emphasized the fact that their system would be enlarged and enriched by new scientific discoveries. Unfortunately for Reich, in the meantime the growth of Marxism had been arrested, and the theory used to justify the bureaucratic reign in the USSR.

We have little information at our disposal about Reich's personality. The people who knew him during his first period and who are still alive are scattered around the world. We can however attempt to build a picture of the man through his work and through a few personal accounts.

Reich was gifted with an exceptional work capacity. He had reached the peak of his scientific career in 1934, when he was only thirty-seven. He wrote all his important books between 1925 and 1934, not counting the scores of articles which he published in the reviews of the Psychoanalytic Association during those years.

He had had to assimilate an impressive amount of information from sociology, ethnology, economics, history, and politics. Knowing how active a militant he was, one wonders when he found the time to write. For example, founding and developing the Sexual Politics Association took up a lot of time and work. Naturally, theory and practice are related; Reich's work was based on his medical observations and what he learned by taking part in political struggles. The orgasm theory, for example, is not a philosophical construction, but an interpretation of what Reich had observed in his patients. Nor did his thesis on the sociological function of the family and on sexual repression spring fully developed from his mind. Besides, Reich was very suspicious of philosophy and abstract speculations. This aversion was extremely pronounced and explains to some extent the "positivist" side of his work. A brief anecdote reveals the degree to which metaphysical fabrications irritated him. During the congress in Lucerne a psychoanalyst read a speech on the role of Thanatos in dreams. Reich then asked him if he had actually seen the death instinct appear in dreams. The other replied no; this was simply a theory. "So why are you talking about it?" Reich exclaimed.

His relationship with Freud reveals his intellectual honesty. Unlike the other psychoanalytic dissenters, Reich never denigrated Freud even after their rupture. For many years, he had protested that psychoanalytic thought was degenerating, and he continued to do so after having been excluded from the movement, but although he said repeatedly that Freud was on the wrong track and that he was mistaken in making his theories more palatable to society, he never made any bitter or petty remarks about his old master, whose sincerity, competence, and courage he admired.

On the other hand, Reich's relationship with the rest of the psychoanalysts, many of whom he considered worldly and conventional, had begun to grow stormy in 1927 when he became a Communist, and the conflicts which were smoldering between them finally broke into the open. He was certainly not an easygoing man; he was stubborn, crafty, caustic and could be unusually bad tempered. By 1933, he had crossed swords with all the members of the Psychoanalytic Movement. His relationship with them had deteriorated to such an extent that during the congress in Lucerne he could find no one to speak in his defense.

We can tell a great deal about what the Psychoanalytic Association thought of Reich from one incident which occurred during the congress in Lucerne. After he had been informed of his exclusion, rumor had it that Reich was intending to assault the president of the Association.

Another facet of Reich's personality is revealed by his decisiveness. For example, when the Communists hampered his progress, he broke away from them and founded an independent publishing house, Sexpol Verlag. Or again, once he was fully aware of the ravages wrought by antisexual morality, he did not hesitate to devote a large part of his income to founding the first sexual hygiene centers in Vienna.

Finally, Reichian thought is distinguished by an internal coherence and a sequence of ideas which heralded his second period. There is something slightly disturbing about Reich's theories, everything holds together a little too well, and the way the theses are expressed has the ring of an obsession to it.

During the course of the preceding chapters, I tried to show that the theory of the libido assumed more and more importance in Reich's thinking. In this regard it is of interest to recall that his first lecture, which he gave at the age of twenty-two at a sexology seminar, was devoted to the evolution of the libido concept. He explained to his audience that Freud considered the libido to be the energy of the sexual instinct, not the instinct itself. And Reich, in a reckless flight of oratory, threw in the idea that perhaps it would be possible to measure it one day.

To illustrate this point, he established a parallel between the libido and electricity. It is clear that he was already thinking of sexual tension as a kind of difference of potential within the organism, and he was tempted to take the metaphor even further by thinking of the orgasm as the discharge of a condensor in a resistance; in the same way that an electric circuit is heated by the flow of the current, the fall of sexual tension is accompanied by pleasure. Reich's concept of the sexual act is obviously drawn from an analogy of this kind.

As long as it is used only as an example, that is to say, a voluntarily simplified way of representing a phenomenon, there is no drawback to this line of thought. But Reich allowed himself to be trapped by the images that he used. He began to believe that the organism contained and gave off a certain energy, and he naturally wanted to measure this energy. Reich's concept of the libido shows that his reasoning was very seriously confused, for the term "sexual energy," which is part of psychoanalytic jargon, must be taken in its figurative sense.

In effect, no one has ever seen or touched the libido. The only thing that one can observe is the sexual behavior (for example, the search for a partner, or the exterior signs of excitement). One infers from this behavior the existence of a specific motivation (the libido), but this is a concept and cannot be considered a material reality. Sexual desire is an abstraction which allows us to understand a whole series of attitudes and actions which often take very different forms, but one has to guard against believing that there is something called the libido which exists in the body. Besides, the concept of desire (or need) is only a theoretical construction that psychologists use because it is a convenient way of describing the phenomena they observe.

To clarify these ideas, let us consider the example of thirst. If a rat is deprived of water for a certain period, or if he is only fed dry foodstuffs, or again, if a saline solution is injected into his stomach, the deprivation of water, the administration of dehydrated food, and the concentration of the saline solution make up three independent variables. We then establish that the rat is agitated and increases his activity, that he drinks more, and that he moves more quickly than usual through the experimental mazes in his cage. The level of the rat's activity, the quantity of water he drinks, the time it takes him to run through his maze are three dependent variables. To establish laws ruling the rat's behavior, one must link each independent variable to each dependent variable which gives us 3 x 3 = 9 laws to determine.

On the other hand, if we introduce the hypothesis of an intermediary variable, we reduce the number of laws to six. In effect, thirst varies in terms of the three independent variables, which makes three relations; the behavior of the rat characterized by three dependent variables, varies in its turn in terms of the thirst, which gives us again three relations: 3+3 = 6; we have thus saved three laws. The diagram on page 191 permits us to visualize all this:

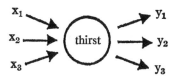

x_1, x_2, x_3: independent variables—y_1, y_2, y_3: dependent variables

For psychologists, the concepts of need and of motivation belong to the intermediary class of variables, which serve to simplify the exposition of theories, but which have no real existence beyond this. Physics and chemistry have a tendency to resort more and more to abstract concepts of this kind in order to understand material phenomena.

We can only evaluate the intensity of the need by the behavior. For example, if we make a rat fast and then put him in front of a piece of cheese from which he is separated by an electrified grid, to "measure the hunger" we count the number of times that the rat is prepared to cross the electrified grid. When we say of a rat who has crossed the grid fifteen times that he is a "very hungry" rat, we are merely employing a figure of speech.

Reich had begun to come off the rails at the moment he tried to see and measure the libido, something which by definition has no material existence. It is exactly as if someone wanted to *bottle* thirst or hunger. Furthermore the inevitable occurred; in 1935, Reich confirmed that he had seen sexual energy, and that it was blue; and in 1938 he maintained that one could accumulate this energy in boxes. He thus threw himself in pursuit of a fantasy and the search lead to madness. But, one asks, if sexual energy is not material, has the orgasm theory any meaning? Reich maintains that neuroses "draw their energy" from the sexual stasis, that is to say, "the quantity of sexual energy which remains dammed up in the organism and which is not released during the orgasm." Now, we have just seen that the expression "sexual energy" must be taken in its figurative sense because it does not exist in the way that one speaks of calorific or kinetic energy.

Fortunately, these reservations do not in any way weaken the orgasm theory. We simply have to interpret "sexual energy" as "sexual excitation" for the orgasm theory to become valid once again. It is sufficient to say that when a human being is sexually excited, he finds himself in a certain physiological and psychological state, and that if he suffers from orgastic impotence this state will persist even after the sexual act. An immediate consequence of orgastic impotence is therefore a permanent state of sexual excitement. Moreover, when Reich used the expression "sexual energy" in 1925, he was conforming to the terminology being used by psychoanalysts.

Reich was always obsessed by the desire to find a biological basis for the theory of the libido. As mammalian sexual behavior is effectively dependent upon hormonal and nervous factors, one can legitimately make a physiological study of sexual life. But that is not what Reich had in mind. He had taken the expression "sexual energy" literally, and he resolved to isolate it. This obsession had certainly been on his mind for a long time before it suddenly found expression in 1934. That year certain changes took place in his personality. He could not bear any criticism and became alarmingly irritable. In 1935 he began slipping into paranoia which soon reached dizzying proportions.

There are several reasons for this tragic turn of events. Evidently one can cite a character predisposition. But there are at least two external factors which played their parts. The first is the central place that the theory of the libido holds in Reich's sociological and psychoanalytic theories. He adopted, augmented, and supported Freud's old fundamental thesis on the crucial importance of sexuality in human conduct. But Freud had given way to Puritan pressure which reproached him for his "pansexualism" while Reich held fast to his theory, hoping to silence his adversaries once and for all, and in so doing, he was obsessed with the need to assemble arguments in support of his viewpoint. This obsession had begun when Freud expressed the hope of seeing the theory of the libido made the object of biological studies. Reich jumped at the idea, but he interpreted it quite wrongly.

The other reason which may explain why Reich's mind finally began to waver is found in the permanent tension he was subjected to from the moment he first formulated his orgasm theory. Without any exaggeration, it can be said that from 1925 Reich lived in an atmosphere of continual polemics and fights. On the intellectual plane, Reich was a kind of tramp, rejected by all the groups to which he belonged. He succeeded in upsetting both the psychoanalysts and Communists at the same time, and his isolation within the two movements was complete by 1932.

In 1933 events gathered speed. Reich had to leave Germany and lead the life of an exile, which was not likely to raise his spirits. His intellectual isolation was doubled by his physical solitude, aggravated by financial difficulties and by harassment from the foreign police. One cannot lead this kind of life with impunity for long. Ten years of conflicts ending in his exclusion from the Party and from the Psychoanalytic Association had turned Reich into a paranoiac. His difficult nature, his violent reactions, alienated him from sympathy which he could have used. From then on, Reich was caught up in a vicious cycle; the more intractable he became, the less people wanted to see him, which added to his solitude and bitterness.

In a passage of his autobiography, *People in Trouble,* he let this cry escape him: "In the space of a few months," he said, "I had lost all my friends."

Chapter XV

The Discovery of the Orgone

Reich had been invited to Oslo by a group of Norwegian psychoanalysts. He arrived at the end of 1934 and stayed until 1939, leading a quiet life devoted entirely to the search for sexual energy. He turned from psychoanalysis, politics, and sociology and immersed himself in the natural sciences. He made fewer contacts with the progressive movement. But he did not cease to associate with them altogether because I found by chance in an edition of the *Anticommunist Review* a note denouncing the Bâle Intellectual Union, which referred to Reich's arrival in 1938. Furthermore, young Nazis, disheartened by the turn that Nazism had taken, came to ask Reich's advice.

While he was still living in Denmark, Reich had begun to move toward an organic treatment of neuroses. He maintained that character armor betrays the presence of a "muscular armor," and that the patient's unconscious resistances are rooted in a muscular rigidity that can actually be felt in his body. For example, he said, if one hits a neurotic unexpectedly in the stomach, he will gasp. According to

Reich, abdominal tension, which never relaxes in neurotics, is evidence of their unconscious defenses. Character resistances are thus riveted in the inflexibility which affects certain selected groups of muscles. There is perhaps some truth in all this. Since the way in which a subject conducts himself is the expression of the sum total of his childhood, how the subject uses his body (the way he breathes, laughs, a stiffness in the way he carries his head, etc.) is significant.

From then on Reich concentrated his therapeutic technique on breaking down the muscular armor and called his new method "vegetotherapy." In a sense he was drawing closer to psychosomatic medicine. He considered that vegetotherapy and character analysis made up the two parts of a single treatment whose immediate goal was the restoration of orgastic potency. It should be pointed out right here that vegetotherapy never caught on.

However, there is no doubt that the muscular armor theory contains a fragment of truth because it has been demonstrated that neurotics suffer somatic repercussions. For example, the psychoanalyst Jung was surprised to discover a high proportion of neuroses among tubercular patients. He was intrigued by this observation until one day he noticed that neurotics breathe in a panting and superficial fashion which does not give the lungs sufficient ventilation.

Vegetotherapy marked a turning point in Reich's thinking. It started the search for sexual energy.

Reich was obsessed with his desire to give evidence of something that had no material existence. His apartment was full of electronic amplifiers, elec-

troscopes, microbic cultures, and biology manuals,
But he did not have a microscope. He got it into his
head that with the help of a powerful microscope he
would be able to see sexual energy. At the end of
1935, one of his students made him a gift of a bi-
nocular (this is a microscope with two eye pieces
which allows one to see in relief) which magnified
to the power of 1,500,000. But first Reich had to
refresh his memory on the use of the microscope because he had not had recourse to one since he was a
medical student in Vienna. Then he went round in
circles for several days wondering how to go about
observing sexual energy, until he had a sudden flash
of understanding. When an animal eats, the energy
contained in the food is assimilated by his organism.
Animal food contains proteins, carbohydrates, and
fats. Thus, Reich reasoned, proteins, carbohydrates,
and fats must contain a "biological energy" which is
probably identical to sexual energy.

He bought meat, vegetables, eggs, and milk, put
them all in a saucepan, and boiled up the mixture for
half an hour. Then he took a drop of this soup and
placed in under the microscope. What he saw on
the slide took his breath away—a myriad of globules
moving in every direction. He immediately came to
the conclusion that these globules were full of biological energy and that he had found what he was
looking for. (In fact he had simply observed an
emulsion, and the vesicles were fat particles in sus-
pension; their agitation was due to Brownian movement).

These vesicles, which Reich said were "charged
with biological energy," he called *bions*. The discovery of the bion dates back to the end of 1935

and the beginning of 1936, marking the first stage of his descent into madness.

The following years were spent furthering his study of these famous bions. He got in touch with bacteriologists hoping to share his enthusiasm, and needless to say he was not very well received. He began to foam and rage, accusing "official science" of deliberately ignoring his discoveries. He treated some of the bacteriologists as if they were congenital psychopaths and questioned the whole science of biology.

He had been trying to persuade the doubting scientists that bions are transformed into microbes and that life can be reborn from inanimate organic matter; in fact he had unearthed the old theory of spontaneous generation, according to which bacteria or protozoa can develop in an aseptic environment.

This theory, which still had partisans in the last century, had been abandoned once and for all after Pasteur's discoveries. We know today with absolute certainty that all living cells must come from other living cells.

For example, when we leave a bottle of milk open, the milk turns sour because microbes are multiplying in the milk, and their metabolic waste is acid, giving spoiled milk its characteristic flavor. If the milk is perfectly sterile, the microbes are carried by the air, which contains the germs of microorganisms. But Reich did not understand this. To him, air was always perfectly pure and never contained any spores. The agents of mildew and microbes which cause putrefaction, he said, come from bions, which develop spontaneously in organic matter.

It is absolutely incomprehensible that Reich could have arrived at a hypothesis of this nature. Every student of bacteriology learns to his cost that air carries germs which can contaminate his cultures. A little later Reich maintained that bions also formed in certain minerals like sand and in cancerous tissue. He cut himself off from all the scientific circles in Oslo and abroad. As he was used to having his ideas rejected by everyone, he was not in the slightest bit disturbed by this latest rebuttal.

He worked day and night in his laboratory and finally got conjunctivitis from peering through his microscope. An idea formed in his mind: perhaps this inflammation of the eye came from radiation emitted by the bions and concentrated by the lens of his microscope. To prove this hypothesis, he submitted himself to all sorts of manipulations and experiments which were proof of a certain ingenuity, if nothing else. He used photographic plates and an electroscope and attached to his skin a tube containing a "culture of bions" to see if it would burn. He came fairly quickly to the conclusion that bions gave off radiation and he baptized this "orgone" energy.

Reich was persuaded that he had made a discovery destined to overthrow biology and medicine. Human beings were charged with orgone energy and when they died their tissues disintegrated forming bions, which developed once again into the elementary forms of life (bacteria and protozoa).

As the scientists ignored him, he began to abuse them and suspect them of having hatched a plot to suppress his discoveries. What is more, he said, modern science has become arid and mechanical because scientists have been ravaged by sexual repres-

sion. This line of attack was extended to psychoanalysts, psychiatrists, and Communists. The texts
Reich wrote at this time are incoherent and their
tone is vehement. No one except Freud found grace
in his eyes. From then on he called Communists
"red Fascists," and accused psychiatrists of being
a band of policemen, bent on confining all neurotics
to concentration asylums. But his favorite target was
the politicians. Reich divided mankind into two
parts: on the one hand were the masses of workers,
conditioned to obey and to submit to authority, and
on the other, were the politicians, who formed a
freemasonry of professional parasites. He drew up a
vague and utopian program to transform the world,
asserting that if we want to put an end to politics,
all those who do productive work (that is, workers,
scientists, farmhands, technicians, etc.) must unite
and govern society. But Reich no longer spoke of
social classes nor of revolutions. Besides he had become more or less nonviolent. He pitted the world
of politicians against the world of workers and
wished that the workers would concentrate on their
work and stop allowing themselves to be influenced
by politics. Politics is in essence irrational, he said.
But on the other hand, what he called "work democracy" (the methods of work organization and
the ties which unite all workers to one another) is
rational. He suggested that work democracy is the
panacea for wars and dictatorships, maintaining that
the state and all political parties are like tumors
growing within the social system. In order to destroy these tumors, the workers must acquire a maturity which they currently lack. The politicians and
diplomats must be sent back to the dressing room of
life, said Reich. Yet he no longer believed in revo-

lution, nor in class struggle, but in spiritual transformation. He invented the following slogan, "Love,
work and knowledge are the wellsprings of our life.
They should also govern it."

All this is well intentioned, but does not lead
very far. Reading his thesis on work democracy, one
becomes aware of the terrible reversion of Reichian
thought after 1935. He was at odds with the whole
world and buried in his laboratory. His magnificent
capacity for work and his superior intelligence were
being sapped by ridiculous experiments and intellectual malnutrition.

He was convinced that all living beings contain
orgone energy and identified the orgone with the
libido. Since his theory raised an infinite number of
objections, he began to transform biology and one
by one all the other natural sciences. One example
among a thousand—Reich had announced that the
energy used by living beings is orgone energy. This
is all very well when applied to animals who eat
vegetables—the orgone contained in their food
crosses the intestinal lining in the form of bions—
but does not explain how plants absorb the orgone
since they have no digestive tract and grow by
drawing minerals up from the soil synthesizing carbohydrates from water and carbon dioxide in the
atmosphere in the presence of sunlight. (A process
called photosynthesis.) By using chemical energy
obtained from the oxidation of glucose, they make
their own proteins and fats.

It did not take Reich long to discover that the
light energy captured by the plants was in reality
orgone energy, and thus the problem was resolved.
Meanwhile, he had ascertained that bions formed
in sand. He then declared that grains of sand were

solid particles of solar energy. In this way he built up an amazing system with an impressive internal coherence. He believed in everything he could prove, and he proved everything he believed. He resolved the problem of the origin of life on earth (thanks to bions which formed the transition between inanimate and animate matter); he could explain the development of cancerous tumors, neuroses, mental illnesses, etc. He discovered that metals reflect orgone energy, just as mirrors reflect light, and that organic substances absorb it. He then built boxes with an external surface composed of wool or cotton and interiors fitted with metal. Thus, he said, if a culture of bions or any living being is put inside the box, the orgone energy will be concentrated within and unable to escape. He looked into the boxes through holes cut in one side, and said that he could see the vibrations. He then conducted a control experiment: he looked into an empty box. To his great surprise, the vibrations persisted despite the absence of an internal source of orgone energy. (This is not in the least surprising because if one stares at a point in the dark for any length of time, one always ends up seeing spots of light.) Reich believed first that the second box had somehow accumulated orgone energy and that if he aired it the light phenomenon would disappear. He cleaned his box, leaving it open for several days in a place where there was no bion culture. Despite these precautions, the shining points remained. He then built another box entirely of metal and put no source of orgone energy in it, but the vibrations persisted. He concluded therefore that the orgone energy trapped in his box could only come from the atmosphere.

He was at this stage in his deductions when he

received an invitation from Dr. Theodore P. Wolfe, an American doctor. The invitation came just in time, for Reich was ready to leave Oslo; he sensed that the war was approaching and the proximity of Nazism was not at all reassuring. Moreover, in his autobiography Reich speaks of a press campaign that the newspapers had conducted against him in 1937. It appears that the articles he was alluding to were directed by doctors against his orgone energy and bion theories. Reich had dreamed up a freakish hypothesis about cancer, which had forced the specialists to put the public on their guard. In brief, a change of air was desirable. In 1939 he permanently left Europe for the United States.

Chapter XVI

The Final Years

Reich arrived in America preceded by a flattering reputation; not only had he been Freud's old assistant, but he was in the company of a number of intellectual Jews who had serious reasons for leaving Germany and seeking a home elsewhere.

From 1939 to 1941 he taught at the New School for Social Research in New York. It did not take him long to surround himself with a coterie of more or less crazy disciples, over whom he exercised a strange fascination. Big modern cities are full of people who are only too ready to believe in table turning or telepathy. With the help of his disciples' funds, Reich set up a laboratory, a publishing house (the Orgone Institute Press) and a magazine (*The Orgone Energy Bulletin*) which published accounts of his experiments. Dr. Theodore P. Wolfe translated practically all Reich's books into English. Unfortunately, Reich adapted them first, taking out passages which no longer suited him, and adding pages on orgone energy. The quality of the texts reflects these changes strongly and it is sometimes difficult to trace the ideas of Reich's "first period" in the books translated and published in the United States.

One of the most far-fetched episodes in Reich's life took place at the beginning of his life in the

United States. On December 30, 1940, he wrote a letter to Einstein, asking if they could meet and informing him that he had discovered a form of energy which opened up new possibilities for the treatment of cancer. He added, probably to forestall an eventual objection from Einstein, that he did not want to send his material to the Academy of Sciences because he had had some very unpleasant experiences with scientists.

A week later, Einstein replied to Reich that he could devote an afternoon to him. The two men agreed to meet on January 13, 1941. The interview lasted for nearly five hours, in the course of which Reich developed his theories on bions and the orgone. Einstein was staggered. After several minutes he realized he was dealing with an eccentric but he let him have his say. When Reich left Einstein, he was sure that the great scientist had rallied to his flag. Overflowing with enthusiasm, he said, "Can you understand now why everyone thinks I'm mad?"

"And how!" Einstein replied imperturbably.

During their meeting, Reich had assured Einstein that one can accumulate orgone energy quite simply by placing a metal box on a table. The proof, he said, is that if you place one thermometer in the box and another under the table on which the box is standing, the two thermometers register different temperatures; the one in the box showing a higher temperature, due to the radiation of orgone energy. Einstein admitted that if the temperature in an enclosed area could be raised without any source of energy, it would be a truly extraordinary discovery.

A few days after this conversation, Reich returned to Einstein's laboratory with an apparatus of thermometers and orgone accumulators and explained to him how he must proceed. Einstein, who throughout this affair showed the patience of an saint, sent Reich his report a week later. He had carried out Reich's experiment and had observed a difference of temperature between the two thermometers. But, he said, there is a very simple explanation for this. Because of the convection current, the air in a room is always a little warmer nearer the ceiling. If one puts a table in the room, warm air from the ceiling is reflected by the superior surface of the table, and in the same way the inferior surface receives cool air reflected from the floor. Given these conditions, explained Einstein, box or no box, we always observe a difference of temperature between two thermometers if one is placed above a table and the other beneath.

At the end of his letter, Einstein advised Reich not to let himself be carried away by an illusion.

Reich replied to Einstein by sending him a long document in which he set forth the essential facts of his orgone theories and an account of his misadventures with the Norwegian biologists. Although Reich badgered him several times, Einstein gave no more sign of life, except for a short letter three years later to assure him that he had nothing to do with certain rumors which accused Reich of charlatanism.

His fanaticism, immense pride, and above all the internal coherence of his system made Reich such a typical paranoiac that his symptoms read like a textbook case from a psychiatry manual. Starting with bions, his theories hang together with strict logic; he had an answer for everything, including the fact that orgone energy had never been discovered before and that no one wanted to recognize its existence. He maintained in effect that the modern world has been made sterile by sexual repression and transformed into an affective desert. Since orgone energy is sexual energy in its pure state, scientists' character armor and their orgastic impotence stop them from seeing something that is staring them in the face.

Nearly all the texts that Reich wrote in the United States were full of self-congratulatory remarks. He explained that his intellectual breadth eclipsed his enemies, who were mere mental defectives. "Reich," he says (he often used the third person in referring to himself), "is an elephant whose enemies have tried to wound him with paper darts." His thirst for recognition took an unpleasant turn when he implied that he should be awarded at least two Nobel prizes, and complacently repeated the remarks to his disciples, who looked upon him as a messiah.

He compared himself to Lenin, Darwin, Freud, and Nietzsche. He announced that he was ready to bring the American government up to date on his discoveries and their possible military application and in every way attempted to attract attention to his works. In a city as tense as New York, Reich had no difficulty recruiting followers. But what is incredible is the number of doctors of medicine and science who allowed themselves to be persuaded by Reich's viewpoint. That Reich was able to convince laymen is one thing, but in the list of collaborators on his magazine we find the names of several professionals. The orgone theory is as farfetched as the notion that the earth is a hollow cube with the sun and stars on the inside.

In 1942, Reich and his disciples bought some

land in Maine. They called this kingdom "Orgonon" and Reich installed a laboratory there where he devoted himself to increasingly outlandish experiments and observations. He was surrounded by oscillographs, cathode-ray tubes, Geiger counters, microscopes, and electrographs. Reich saw orgone energy everywhere—in the sky, in the clouds, in the oceans, in frogspawn. He photographed the northern lights and confirmed that the spiral form of the nebula indicated that it came from two joined orgonic currents sustaining a cosmic orgasm. (We must admit that all this does have its poetic side).

Reich discovered the presence of orgone energy in the atmosphere; the ether whose existence had prompted the physicians of old to explain the transmission of electromagnetic waves. Next he declared that the orgone, the ether, and God were three different names meaning the same thing, thus becoming a sort of pantheist.

He demonstrated that universal gravitation did not exist, and that the stars, the sun, and the planets were floating on an orgone ocean.

He spent some time in the study of hurricanes (with graphs, aerial photos, diagrams, etc.) and concluded that hurricanes, like nebula, were formed by the coming together of two orgone energy flows.

The atmosphere in his home where he was surrounded by his disciples must have been peculiar. He worked enormously hard, devouring books on astrophysics, chemistry, and biology, pouncing on each passage which appeared to support his theories. He performed a number of bizarre experiments which would be tedious to describe, but one of them appears to have gone wrong because several of Reich's collaborators suddenly fell ill (including his seven-year-old son) and had to be evacuated swiftly. A short time before, Reich had bought some radium to see what would happen if one placed radioactive energy in the presence of orgone energy.

Reich walked about at night contemplating the heavens, that huge ocean of orgone energy, and dreaming of far-off galaxies. His thoughts took a mystical turn and he wrote a strange work titled *The Murder of Christ,* where poems were alternated with commentaries on the life of Jesus and bitter attacks against politicians. Evidently Reich was identifying with Christ and thought of himself as the new messiah. He said that Christ's message to the world had not been heard. He had railed against the hypocrites and the envious; he had lived the life of an anarchistic wanderer refusing to bow to social convention; and he had spread abroad his message of universal love, social equality, and the rejection of authority. What is more, he had refused to establish a political party, preferring to believe that his ideas could be spread peacefully.

On his arrival in the United States, Reich had taken out a patent for an orgone energy accumulator to be used therapeutically. It was a metallic cabin surrounded by wood, in which he made his patients sit. The object of the exercise was the following: The orgone energy radiated by his patients was reflected by the metal sides of the accumulator, concentrated in the apparatus, and repenetrated the body through the skin and through respiration. Reich put these accumulators on the market, assuring his buyers that they cured cancer, schizophrenia, colds, etc.

Evidently, this claim bordered on charlatanism.

But the profits which came from the sale of the accumulators was reinvested in "research," and Reich was persuaded that they really did cure disease. It would be wrong to think of him as a profiteer. On the contrary, Reich had always shown himself to be generous and disinterested in money, which was to his credit. In Vienna and in Berlin, he spent a good part of his income in renting halls for the Communist youth or in publishing brochures for the Sexual Politics Association. When he was forced to escape from Berlin, he did not even have enough money to take the train.

In 1954, things grew worse. As a rule, no medication can be put on the American market without the approval of the U.S. Food and Drug Administration, whose job is to control foodstuffs and pharmaceutical products. As the success of the orgone accumulators grew, even psychiatrists and doctors bought them to heal their patients. Reich received orders from the United States, Europe, and Palestine. This finally attracted the attention of the FDA, which brought an action against Reich and the Wilhelm Reich Foundation (the association created in 1949 by Reich's disciples).

Reich refused to appear before the court and sent a letter to the judge explaining that the field of his research was situated beyond the judicial domain and that in these circumstances the law did not concern him. "Besides," he added, "my discovery is widely known nearly all over the globe. It can no longer be stopped by anyone." On March 19, 1954, judgment was passed. It was severe; and it is permissible to wonder if political or psychological motives had not inspired the trial in the first place. Reich was an erstwhile Communist, and even after he reached the United States, he had not ceased attacking the family institution.

Reich was enjoined:

1. to withdraw all his orgone accumulators from the market and to destroy them;
2. to burn all texts, articles, and reviews concerning the construction and use of the orgone accumulators;
3. to withdraw from the market *all his books,* whose sale was henceforth prohibited.

One can understand why justice had to intervene in the matter of the orgone accumulators. On the other hand, the banning of all his books (including *The Mass Psychology of Fascism, The Sexual Revolution, Character Analysis*) had nothing to do with orgone accumulators. It is true that Reich had slipped some paragraphs on the orgone into certain of these works, which was the reason given by the judge, but it is clear that this was only a pretext to hinder the spread of Reich's revolutionary doctrine.

Reich ignored the court ruling, which brought about a second trial in May 1956. This time he pleaded not guilty and was condemned to two years in prison; the Reich Foundation was fined ten thousand dollars; all Reich's books were withdrawn from circulation; and his magazine and orgone accumulators were burnt in the presence of two FDA representatives.

Reich was imprisoned on March 11, 1957, in the Federal Penitentiary at Lewisburg in Pennsylvania. He died there eight months later, on November 3, 1957.

There are certain things that society permits us to think about but forbids us to do. We don't give a damn about society.

It:

- stops us from satisfying our needs.

- confines us to masturbation.

- tells us that "good girls" don't sleep around.

- permits the circulation of erotic pictures in films and advertisements which excite us, but forbids us to seek sexual satisfaction, and calls this pornography "culture" into the bargain.

We:

- should like sexual freedom without regard to established laws and moral precepts.

- should like to be free of guilt and live according to our desires and aspirations.

- don't want boys to have intercourse with prostitutes, nor girls to be abstinent. We want intercourse with one another.

- don't want to make love on the quiet, but to do it in comfort neither being ashamed nor interrupted.

Young people have more than the simple right to information, they have every right to realize their sexuality. This right has been taken away.

The young must take their fate into their own hands if they want to put a stop to the misery about which they talk so much.

WE DO NOT ASK FOR OUR RIGHTS, WE FIGHT FOR THEM.

[Tract found in Nanterrein 1967.]

Chronology

1897 Wilhelm Reich born into a German farming family in Galicia.

1915 Mobilized in Austrian Army. Lieutenant at war's end.

1918 Enrolled in the Medicine Faculty at the University of Vienna.

1920 Became a member of the Vienna Psychoanalytic Society. Began to practice psychoanalysis.

1922 Received the title of Doctor of Medicine. Started a psychoanalytic practice. Became Freud's assistant at the psychoanalytic polyclinic.

1924 Became director of the psychotherapy seminar at the polyclinic.

1927 Entered the Austrian Communist Party.

1928 Became vice director of the Psychoanalytic polyclinic. Opened the sexual hygiene centers (Sozialistiche Gesellschaft für Sexualberatung und Sexualforschung).

1929 Traveled to USSR.

1930 Moved to Berlin; gave courses in the psycho-analytic clinic of Berlin and at the German Communist Party's Workers University.

1931 Opened Sexual Politics Association. Became an activist in German Communist Party.

1932 Relationship with the Communist Party leaders became strained.

1933 Nazis came to power forcing him to escape from Germany. Reich sought refuge first in Vienna then in Denmark. Open conflict with the International Psychoanalytic Association.

1934 Expelled from Psychoanalytic Association. Settled in Oslo, Norway.

1936 "Discovery" of bions.

1939 "Discovery" of cosmic orgone. Reich leaves for U.S.A.

1942 Foundation of Orgone Institute in New York. Bought land in Rangeley, Maine.

1954 Reich prosecuted by the Federal Food and Drug Administration. Found guilty in his absence. Disregarded the sentence.

1956 Second trial. Reich condemned to two years in jail.

1957 Died in Lewisburg Penitentiary. Age 60.

Bibliography

By Wilhelm Reich:

Der Triebhafte Charakter. Wien: International Psychoanalytischer Verlag, 1925.
Der Sexuelle Kampf der Jugend. Berlin: Sexpol Verlag, 1932.
Der Urgegensatz des Vegetativen Lebens. Copenhagen: Sexpol Verlag, 1934.
Dialektischer Materialismus und Psychoanalyse. Copenhagen: Sexpol Verlag, 1934.
Der Einbruch der Sexualmoral, 2. Auflage. Oslo: Sexpol Verlag, 1935.
Psychischer Kontakt und Vegetative Strömung. Copenhagen: Sexpol Verlag, 1935.
Experimentelle Ergebnisse über die Elektrische Funktion von Sexualität und Angst. Copenhagen: Sexpol Verlag, 1937.
Die Bione. Oslo: Sexpol Verlag, 1938.
The Sexual Revolution. New York: Orgone Institute Press, 1945; Farrar, Straus & Giroux (paperback), 1962.
The Mass Psychology of Fascism. New York: Farrar, Straus & Giroux (hardback and paperback), 1970.
The Cancer Biopathy. New York: Orgone Institute Press, 1948.
The Function of the Orgasm, 2nd Edition. New York:

Orgone Institute Press, 1948; Farrar, Straus & Giroux, 1961.

Listen, Little Man! New York: Orgone Institute Press, 1948; Farrar, Straus & Giroux, (paperback), 1965.

Character Analysis, 3rd Enlarged Edition. New York: Orgone Institute Press, 1949; Farrar, Straus & Giroux (paperback), 1961.

Ether, God and Devil. New York: Orgone Institute Press, 1949.

Cosmic Superimposition. Rangeley, Me.: The Wilhelm Reich Foundation, 1951.

The Oranur Experiment. Rangeley Me.: Orgone Institute Press, 1951.

The Orgone Energy Accumulator. Rangeley, Me.: Orgone Institute Press, 1951.

The Murder of Christ. Rangeley Me.: Orgone Institute Press, 1953; Farrar, Straus & Giroux (paperback), 1956, 1966.

People in Trouble. Rangeley, Me.: Orgone Institute, Press, 1953.

Selected Writings. New York: Farrar, Straus & Cudahy, 1960.

The Invasion of Compulsory Sex-Morality. New York: Farrar, Straus & Giroux, 1971.

Contact With Space: Oranur Second Report, 1951–56. New York: Core Pilot Press.

Orgone Institute Press Publications:
International Journal of Sex-Economy and Orgone Research. New York, 1942–45.
Annals of the Orgone Institute. New York, 1947.
Orgone Energy Bulletin. New York, 1949–55.
Orgonomic Medicine, New York, 1955, 1966.

Baker, Elsworth F. **Man in the Trap.** New York: Macmillan, 1967.

Constandse, Anton. **Sexualiteit en Levensleer: de Sexuele en Politieke Psychologie van Dr. W. Reich.** Antwerp: Uitgeverij "Het Lichtschip," 1938.

Freud, Sigmund. **An Autobiographical Study.** London: Hogarth Press, 1946; W.W. Norton (paperback), 1963.

————. **Basic Writings.** New York: Random House, 1938.

————. **Beyond The Pleasure Principle.** New York: Bantam (paperback), 1959; Liveright Publishing Corporation, 1961.

————. **Civilization and Its Discontents.** New York: W.W. Norton (hardback and paperback), 1962.

————. **Complete Introductory Lectures.** New York: W.W. Norton, 1966.

————. **The Ego and the Id,** 4th Edition. London: Hogarth Press, 1946; W.W. Norton (paperback), 1962.

Higgins, Mary, and Raphael, Chester M., M.D., Editors. **Reich Speaks of Freud.** New York: Farrar, Straus & Giroux, 1967.

Horney, Karen. **New Ways in Psychoanalysis.** New York: W.W. Norton, 1939; (paperback), 1966.

Malinowski, Bronislaw. **Sex and Repression in Savage Society.** London: Routledge & Keegan Paul, 1953; Meridian (paperback), 1960.

Neill, A.S., and others. **Wilhelm Reich.** Edited by Paul Ritter. Nottingham, England: The Ritter Press, 1958.

Orgonomic Publications. **The Journal of Orgonomy.** New York: 1967, 1968.

Reich, Ilse Ollendorff. **Wilhelm Reich: A Personal Biography.** New York: St. Martin's Press, 1969; Avon (paperback), 1970.

Robinson, Paul A. **The Freudian Left: Wilhelm Reich, Geza Roheim, Herbert Marcuse.** New York: Harper & Row, 1969.

Wolfe, Theodore P. **Emotional Plague versus Orgone Biophysics.** New York: Orgone Institute Press, 1948.

Index

Abortions, 78, 95-97
Abraham, Karl, 185
Abstinence, myth of, 96-99, 158
Adler, Alfred, 44
Adolescent sexuality: Communist Party and, 155-60; family and, 94-103, 112-13; neurosis and, 86-92
Adorno, T. W., 127-28
Adultery, 96, 100, 134
Advertising, 115
Affection, sexuality and, 102-3
Aggression, 37-39, 69
Anabolism, 66
Anal phase, 16
Anal sadism, 143
Analysis, inadequacies of, 39-41
Animal behavior, conflicts and, 19-21
Animal Drive and the Learning Process (Holt), 71
Anticommunist Review, 195
Anxiety, neuroses and, 43, 45
Armor: character, 45-52, 126-30; muscular, 195-96; *see also* Resistance
Association for Sexual Politics, 127, 150-63
Authoritarian ideologies, 110
Authoritarian personality, 127-30
Authoritarianism, family and, 104-13
Anthropologists, family studies of, 80-82
Austro-Hungarian Empire, ethnic composition of, 7

Autoeroticism, 16

Bachofen, Johann Jacob, 103, 130, 131
Bâle Intellectual Union, 195
Barash (Russian doctor), 99
Behavior: character structure and, 41-52; irrational mass, 114-37
Bernfeld, Siegfried, 140
Beyond the Pleasure Principle (Freud), 63-65, 67, 69, 72
Biological energy, 197
Bions, discovery of, 197-99
Bolshevism: Freud's view of, 82-84; sexual repression and, 137
Bourgeois society, *see* Society
Brutality, police, 75-76, 87

Cancer, Reich's cure for, 203, 205-6
Capitalism, mass behavior and, 114-37
Castration complex, 18, 49
Catabolism, 66
Catharsis, 38
Causality, 69
Character: analysis of, 36-52; structure of, 44-47
Character Analysis (Reich), 37, 52
Character armor, 45-52, 126-30
Character neuroses, 46-51
Chastity, 96-98
Children: family and, 80-81; molesters of, 144; neuroses and, 86-92; proletarian, 79;

219